With regards
Robert J. Little
Acts 27:25

INSIGHT

By

ROBERT J. LITTLE

MOODY PRESS

CHICAGO

Library of Congress Catalog Card Number: 77-155697

Printed in the United States of America

FOREWORD

Our age wants to know the answers, and we as believers are responsible to provide them.

The Bible plainly challenges us to be "ready always to give an answer to every man that asketh you a reason of the hope that is in you with meekness and fear" (1 Pe 3:15).

Knowing the scriptural answers fortifies our own faith as well as equips us to intelligently share with our fellowman.

Radio Pastor Robert J. Little has given his life to the ministry of providing biblical answers to perplexing questions of our times. This book is a must for pastors and laymen alike.

GEORGE SWEETING
President, Moody Bible Institute

PREFACE

This book is a compilation of discussions given originally on the "Moody Presents" program of the Moody Bible Institute. They were aired over a large number of stations in various parts of the country. Since the subjects were not linked sequentially when originally given, their compilation in that form has resulted in a certain amount of overlapping of references. However, it was thought best to leave each discussion in its original form rather than rewrite them; and it is hoped that the repetitions will have the effect of causing them to become fastened in the mind and memory of the reader. Meantime, the reader's indulgence is requested and gratefully acknowledged by the author.

CONTENTS

GOD AND THE BIBLE

How Do We Know There Is a God?

With man's increasing knowledge of science and technocracy, it is not uncommon for people to question the existence of God. How do we know there is a God?

1

That is a good question because even believers sometimes have doubts. The question is sometimes raised by persons who believe in no god at all. Also those whose religion involves a multiplicity of gods ask why our God should be accepted as the only true God. Can we prove the validity of the one and disprove the value of the others? In a large segment of society idols are worshiped. The prophet Isaiah in several passages discusses the impotence of idols, pointing out that they are made by man, sometimes from a tree the balance of which has been used for firewood. He also points out that they must be moved about and fastened so they won't fall, and he argues their inability to help. We can smash them or burn them or melt them down, depending on their composition. But one who worships idols might retort: "You have less. You close your eyes and pray to nothing. How can you be sure there is a God who listens and is able to help?" Yet the basic demand of Christian belief is that "he that cometh to God must believe that he is, and that he is a rewarder of them that diligently seek him" (Heb 11:6).

Does this mean that we must assume the existence of God without any substantial evidence of His existence?

2

No. There is substantial evidence of the existence of God, both negative and positive. On the negative side, if we adopt the proposition that there is no God, we are confronted with the

existence of a highly organized creation which must be considered either to have existed eternally or to have come into
existence by spontaneous creation, that is, it brought itself into
being. And if we assume that this creation was in a crude form,
we must conclude that without the aid of any outside force or
intelligence, the universe developed itself into increasingly complex forms. Were that the case, then that would be the kind of
universe in which we live, where things spring into existence out
of nothing, without the assistance of any previously existing force
or intelligence and where things constantly develop into more
complex forms. But the experience of humanity has been the
reverse. There is a law of deterioration, and things left to themselves usually resolve themselves back into a more primitive state.

A strong argument against the evolution of higher biological
forms from lower is that many of the features of the more complex forms of life would be useless unless fully formed and
operative in conjunction with other complex features of which
they are a part. They would, in fact, in an incomplete or im-
mature form be a detriment. Hence on the theory of the survival
of useful development these would be rejected and would never
come to fulfillment.

3   What are some of the positive proofs of the existence of God?

For those who are willing to accept the eternity of matter it
should be no great problem to accept an eternal God with sufficient wisdom and power to bring the universe into being and
to order it in the complexity of forms in which we find it. A
biblical argument for the existence of God is found in Hebrews
3:4: "Every house is builded by some man [someone]; but he
that hath built all things is God." This is the argument that
design requires a designer. One could give many illustrations of
this. If we look at the winding course of a river or the irregular
line of a canyon, no one supposes that these were the work of an
architect or builder. But where we find formed bricks or dressed
stone—and especially where these are placed in a defined order,
as in a wall or other structure—anyone must admit that this
required the presence of some human designer. No one would
claim that such a result was the product of the forces of nature,

such as wind, sun, and so on. If we see a footprint we know
someone made it, even though the one who made it was not seen
or even known to have been there. So it has been said that the
ordered system of the universe, making possible calculations
enabling man to travel in space, is in a sense a footprint of God.

Psalm 19 gives us a poetical statement of the fact that creation
is a witness to the existence of the Creator. The apostle Paul
states that this witness is the basis for the condemnation of those
who do not believe: "The invisible things of him [God] from the
creation of the world are clearly seen, being understood by the
things that are made, even his eternal power and Godhead; so
that they are without excuse" (Ro 1:20).

**This shows the existence of God, but how can we know He is   4
interested in the individual?**

There are both a presumptive proof and a more specific one.
In nature two major areas display the wonders of creation. One
of these is what we call space, sometimes called the telescopic
world, which includes not only our solar system but a vast ex-
panse of galaxies beyond. On the other hand there is the micro-
scopic world in which we find a marvelous display of wisdom in
the organization of minute creatures, and this extends to the
structure of the atom itself. The snowflake is an example of
beauty and intricacy of design even in something of such limited
duration. Every snowflake is constructed on a hexagonal design;
yet, a man who had photographed thousands of them stated that
he did not find two precisely alike. This gives presumptive proof
that the God who is interested in the vastness of space is equally
concerned with the most infinitesimal part of it.

Is there a more specific proof of this?   5

Yes, in the Bible. The Lord Jesus referred to this by declaring
that even a sparrow shall not fall to the ground without the
Father (Mt 10:29), and He added: "Fear ye not therefore, ye are
of more value than many sparrows." The context indicates that
God is not only concerned with each of us individually but with
everything that concerns us. It has been suggested that our
finger- and footprints are divinely appointed since, so far as is

known, no two persons have ever had the same prints. There is substantial evidence, not only of the existence of God, but of His concern for mankind and for every member of the human race.

Must We Accept the Bible as the Word of God?

6   Does Christianity require that we accept the Bible as an inspired revelation from God?

Yes. The basis of Christianity is Christ, His person and work, but our knowledge of Christ and His work depends on the record we have in the Bible. Without it we would be left to tradition and hearsay, and this would be a flimsy foundation on which to rest for our relationship to God for eternity. If we believe there is a God who made us, and to whom we must give account of our lives, it is to be expected that He would give us an authoritative revelation on which to base our faith and by which we may know His will for our lives. The Bible claims to be such a divinely inspired revelation, and we believe its claims can be sustained.

7   What are some of the proofs that the Bible is a revelation from God?

The evidences are numerous. One is its unique style. The Bible speaks as a divine oracle. The writers or speakers whose words are recorded often affirm: "Thus saith the Lord." The nature of the contents of the Bible is such that one gets the sense of a personal message from God; and it not only reveals God's thoughts to us but has the strange faculty of exposing our inward attitudes. The substance of the Bible is likened to many things. It is said to be like food and water—like bread and milk and meat. It is said to be like a hammer and fire. A fire serves various functions—it warms us and cooks our food; but it also consumes— sometimes dross and refuse, but at other times that which we cherish. A hammer can be used to construct something, but it can also be used destructively. The Bible is also likened to a mirror. Sometimes it reveals the one who looks into it, though from another angle Another looks out; that is to say, as we study the Bible, we find in it a reflection of the Son of God, the Lord Jesus Christ. A mirror reveals our need of cleansing, but unlike an ordinary mirror, the Bible reveals our need for inward (spiritual) cleansing, and it also provides the means to accomplish this. Water not only refreshes us as we drink but cleanses as we bathe.

Are there other proofs of the inspiration of the Bible? 8

Yes. While these we have mentioned show its usefulness and relevancy in human experience, they do not guarantee its accuracy and validity. It is a striking fact that the Bible is unlike the literature of its time in that it has retained currency throughout the centuries and millennia since it was first written and has not had to be revised because of scientific absurdities. In fact *scientific thought* has changed frequently on various subjects, and while the Bible is not a treatise on any scientific subject, it does not contain statements which contradict any known fact of science today. This shows divine superintendence in its writing, especially since among its human writers were men of no great learning.

Another evidence of divine inspiration is the unity of subject matter though the Bible was written over a period of more than 1,500 years, by various writers as disparate as kings and peasants, including some who were herdsmen and shepherds with little or no training in the arts and sciences, or even in theology. Yet their contributions to the Bible have added up to a harmonious whole, so that it is possible to make cross references as though the whole were the work of one author. This confirms the superintendence of the Holy Spirit in inspiring the authors, though the perception of this unity requires the discipline of study, as would be required for an adequate knowledge of any other subject, such as mathematics, medicine, or sociology.

Is there a more specific proof of the inspiration and authority of the Bible? 9

The fulfillment of prophecy is claimed in the Bible itself to be evidence of the existence of God and that the Bible is the product of divine inspiration. The prophet Isaiah, in opposing the idolatry of his day, showed the impotence of idols as being the product of man's ingenuity and workmanship, having no power in themselves. They had to be fashioned by man, transported to where they were to be set up, and then fastened so they would not fall (Is 44:9-20; 46:1-7). In contrast Isaiah claimed there is a living God who made us and sustains and strengthens us and who is able to give help in time of need. As a proof of the validity of his claim to speak for this living and true God, Isaiah pointed to fulfilled prophecy and challenged the priests of the idols to match this with prophecies of their own. In 44:6-8 Isaiah emphasizes that no other deity can accurately predict the future. This is repeated in 45:19-22 and again in 46:9-11.

10 Could not the fulfillment of prophecy be a chance coincidence, perhaps based on the law of probability?

This is the case with prophecies which are not divinely inspired. They are sometimes fulfilled, usually in keeping with the laws of probability. But the prophecies of Scripture often run contrary to the laws of probability, with the added complication that often several prophecies relate to the same circumstance, making coincidence altogether unlikely. Any single prophecy has an even chance of being fulfilled. But when twenty-five details are given about a single event, the chance of fulfillment by coincidence becomes one in more than thirty million, making it virtually nil. Hence the fulfillment of so many diverse prophecies in the circumstances of the birth, life, and death of Christ constitutes a striking proof of divine foreknowledge and power in the giving of them. This goes to prove the existence of God, the authenticity of the Bible, and the validity of the claims of Christ.

An example of prophecy running counter to probability is seen in God's choice of Mary, a resident of Nazareth, to be our Lord's mother; yet, He was to be born in Bethlehem. Luke 2 shows how God brought about the fulfillment of the prophecy. With regard to Christ's death, several examples could be given. The description of His death in Psalm 22 required crucifixion. The gospel records show that though the Jews condemned Jesus to death, instead of stoning Him, they delivered Him to the Romans to carry out the execution. Thus every detail was fulfilled. Also, Pilate gave orders that the legs of those crucified that day should be broken, but Christ was excepted, again fulfilling prophecy. Instead His side was pierced, fulfilling yet another prophecy. The circumstances permit no other explanation than divine foreknowledge and superintendence.

Have Succeeding Revisions Altered the Bible Message?

If the Bible is inspired, why has it been revised from time to time?   11

It should be noticed that it is not the basic text of the Bible which has been revised but various translations of it. Revisions, in fact, far from altering or correcting the basic text of the Bible, represent an effort to get nearer to that text. With the passing of time, the usages of words change in any living language. Consequently what might have been a valid translation at the time it was made becomes obsolete for various reasons. Sometimes words ceased to be used at all. For instance, how many today would know what a "habergeon" is? Sometimes grammatical constructions cease to be valid. Today we would not use the expression: "Against Joseph came at noon." Also some words change their meaning, and sometimes take on quite the opposite meaning. "Let" used to mean to hinder. Now it means to allow. "Prevent" originally meant to go before. Now it means to hinder. So there are many instances where the wording of the King James Version does not accurately convey the sense of the original writing. Such things make revision imperative—not with any thought of altering the original sense of the Bible but in order to communicate its revelation in an intelligible and authentic way.

12   Scholars sometimes speak of a "better text." Does this mean that there are various texts from which one may choose what he considers most acceptable?

This refers to various copies of the Bible. Although the Bible has had currency from the time of its writing, beginning before 1400 B.C., none of its original manuscripts are extant. However there exist numerous copies which were made at various times. Since in early times these were all made by hand, it was inevitable that some mistakes should have been made in copying. Sometimes marginal notes were copied into the text on the mistaken assumption that they were part of the text. At other times a copyist inadvertently omitted a word or a phrase or perhaps a line. The end result was a number of variations in different texts. However there is such a mass of material available, much of it dating from very ancient times, that we can be reasonably sure of the substance of the text; and it is an interesting fact that no important doctrine or teaching of Christianity rests on a questionable text.

When a scholar speaks of a "better text" or the "best text," he is stating his belief, supported by numerous manuscripts, that a certain reading is more likely to be the original writing than certain other manuscript readings. A tremendous amount of research has been done in the field of Bible manuscripts, and recent discoveries of some ancient copies of parts of Scripture dating back to the time of Christ have helped to confirm that the Bible we have today is substantially the same as that accepted as Holy Scripture in the time of Christ.

13   In view of these differences, can we consider that our English Bible is inspired?

Yes, if we keep in mind the difference between the verbal inspiration of the original text and the fact that no translation has that kind of authentication. This accounts for different translations expressing things differently, though sometimes this is due to a translator's departing from the text itself and introducing interpretation of meaning rather than translating the text itself. Many factors are involved which can not be discussed in a limited scope. In some cases a translator is admittedly giving a paraphrase, which may impart fresh meaning to a passage, although the danger here lies in that when we depart from what God actually *said*, we lose the fine balance between divine revelation and divine inspiration. God not only gave *concepts* to the writers of Scripture but also guided them in communicating the ideas He revealed. A paraphrase expresses concepts in words which, while they may stimulate and refresh, are not divinely inspired and may prove to be less permanent than the words God chose. But translating does involve communicating concepts and is not simply rendering words and grammar into another language. Perhaps we can say that paraphrases are helpful to stimulate our thinking, while our theological concepts and doctrines should be formed from a more literal rendering of the original texts.

How can we know that a particular translation is reliable? 14

This, of course, results from intensive study. As with any field of learning, we cannot expect to have an adequate grasp of it unless we apply ourselves to it. The Bible is the communication to us of God's mind and will, and it merits all the study we can give it. It has been the subject of the research of many scholars over the centuries, and much of what they have gleaned has been put in writing, so that there is a vast library of written material available to help in various aspects of Bible study. It is helpful to have some acquaintance with at least part of this material, so as to be able to form a reasonable judgment of what is reliable and what is not. But there is also a mass of material which we believe to be unsatisfactory and unreliable. A course of study in a Bible school or correspondence courses from a dependable school could be very helpful in this connection.

Does this mean that no one can understand the Bible unless he is a scholar? 15

No, by no means. The paramount requisite for understanding the Bible is to be taught by the Holy Spirit. One might be a scholar and not be led by the Spirit or even born of the Spirit. On the other hand, one might be led by the Holy Spirit even though not a scholar. In 1 Corinthians 2:7-15 are listed three important steps involved in our receiving a communication from

God through the Bible. First, the concept is communicated by revelation. This is then committed to writing through the inspiration of the Holy Spirit. And third, we must be born of the Spirit and taught by Him in order to understand the truth revealed. The Bible is constantly said to be the test of our ideas, and this is why it is so important to give ourselves to its study. It is not only a source of knowledge but the authority which governs our lives. The Lord Jesus said, "Man shall not live by bread alone, but by every word that proceedeth out of the mouth of God" (Mt 4:4). We not only study it, but we live by it.

Should I Read the Bible If I Do Not Understand It?

16   To many people the Bible doesn't make sense; should they read it anyway?

Since the Bible is God's authentic revelation of Himself and of His mind and will for man, it behooves everyone to read it. If we read the Bible with the desire to understand its meaning and with the intention of obeying its instructions, we have the assurance that the Holy Spirit will help us to understand it. Some insist that the Bible can be understood only by scholars, and in particular by clergymen, and that it is presumptuous and dangerous for so-called laymen to read the Bible for themselves. We believe this idea is fallacious, and it has been abandoned to a large extent in recent years. The Bible is not written in technical language but is intended for ordinary people. At the conclusion of his letter to the Thessalonians, the apostle Paul said, "I charge you by the Lord that this epistle be read unto all the holy brethren" (1 Th 5:27). He also instructed the Colossian church to read certain of his letters to the entire church. Perhaps the book of Revelation is one of the most difficult of the New Testament books to understand, and yet we read: "Blessed is he that readeth, and they that hear the words of this prophecy, and keep those things which are written therein" (1:3). Reading and hearing and obeying are stressed, rather than having complete understanding of all that is contained in the book.

Can we do anything to help in the understanding of the Bible?   17

First of all, in order to gain insight into the meaning of the Bible, it is of the utmost importance that we know the Lord Jesus Christ by faith in Him and that we have submitted ourselves to Him as our Lord and Saviour. Yet even one who is a stranger to God will be led by the Holy Spirit if he reads the Bible to learn the way of salvation. The Bible claims to be written by divine inspiration, and so its meaning can be understood only by the illumination of the Holy Spirit (1 Co 2:12-16). If we have trusted in Christ, the Holy Spirit dwells within us, and we can count on His guidance, though this does not mean that we automatically understand the Bible all at once. He guides us as we study it.

For anyone to try to understand the Bible before he knows Christ in a personal way is difficult and often unsatisfying. In my own case I could not even understand its grammar; yet, when I came to know Christ as my Saviour, I had an intense desire to study the Bible and found great delight and benefit in doing so. Someone spoke of finding a certain book uninteresting until he met the author. Then he read it with pleasure and profit. So it is with the Bible; it takes on meaning and interest when we know Christ personally. It becomes the food of our souls, and we receive instruction from it and are strengthened by its promises.

Are there any simple guidelines which will help one who has not   18 had the benefit of formal Bible study?

We suggest starting with one of the gospels, perhaps Mark or John, which will give some idea of the life and ministry of Christ. The epistle to the Romans is perhaps the most cogent statement of Christian doctrine to be found in the Bible. The Psalms are experiential, and while one might not at first understand all the historical and prophetical implications, he would find much to comfort him in trial; and they contain many precious promises to the one who endeavors to walk by faith and not by sight.

It is good practice to follow some systematic form of Bible reading, perhaps a chapter a day, or even half a chapter if it is long, and to read through the whole Bible. Those who have tried this, asking the guidance of the Holy Spirit, have often been amazed to find many things becoming clear as they go along. When questions arise as you read through the Scriptures, jot them down and try to find an answer, either in Bible study helps or expositions or in conversation with other Christians. Often others who have never thought about the particular question may be stimulated. And if they have already found an answer, they can help you. This also helps develop Christian fellowship.

19 Does the Old Testament have equal authority with the New?

Yes. "Every word of God is pure," we read in Proverbs 30:5, and nothing that God has put in His Word shall ever fail of fulfillment. However much of the Old Testament is history, and much of it is prophecy. All this must be understood, for such sections may not have direct application to us today, though they help us to understand the ways and dealings of God in the past, present and future. There are also various "dispensations," or God's modes of dealing with various men at various times; and if these are not taken into account we may try to apply literally to us something which had to do with a previous dispensation and the value of which lies in its typical teaching. The epistle to the Hebrews shows that the entire Old Testament ritual—with its temple, priesthood, and offerings—while carried out literally in the past dispensation, was at the same time typical of certain spiritual truths in this dispensation. Hence the Old Testament has a distinct value for us, even though we do not carry it out literally today. Besides, the Old Testament contains many spiritual lessons which are not confined to any particular dispensation.

20 Is the Bible to be taken literally?

Parts of the Bible are obviously written in symbolic language, for example, Ezekiel's vision of the cherubim. The book of Revelation is declared to be communicated in symbolic language (1:1), and it contains much that must be taken in this way. An example is the description of Christ in 1:12-20. To take such passages literally would only discredit the Bible. Yet there is much in the Bible which we believe *is* to be taken literally. A rule has been suggested that when the plain sense makes common sense, we should seek no other sense. Also, many things which were rightly taken literally at a given time are found to have symbolic or allegorical meaning as well. It is interesting to see in how many passages of the Bible such explanations are given and such applications made. This all develops as we become increasingly familiar with the subject matter of the Bible, both by reading the Book itself and by taking advantage of the various Bible study helps which are available.

Why Doesn't God Do Something?

Since God is omnipotent, why does He not intervene to bring 21
peace on earth?

It is a question of timing. The Bible predicts there will be a time of reformation or rectification (Heb 9:10). Peter speaks of it as "the times of restitution of all things, which God hath spoken by the mouth of his holy prophets since the world began" (Ac 3:21). These prophecies go far beyond anything men usually think of. Many persons think that if nations would stop warring and populations would stop rioting, then we could enjoy life. Each person could "do his thing," as circumstances might permit. For many, this would mean continuing in sin, indulging in pleasures which are harmful to body and soul. Such pleasures often result in harm to others, and this would destroy the very conditions we all desire.

Many people would be glad if God would restrain the violence and evil of others and allow *them* to continue in their own indulgences. They often justify this by rationalizing that their sins are not as serious as those of the ones they think God should restrain. But when God deals with sin, He will do so with everyone, not just a few. It is only when society as a whole is ordered in righteousness that we can have universal peace. "The work of righteousness shall be peace, and the effect of righteousness quietness and assurance forever" (Is 32:17).

22   What are some of the conditions foretold in prophecy?

One has been quoted many times. It is a condition for which
men long and strive and which they cannot achieve, because they
seek it apart from God. It occurs twice in the Bible: "They shall
beat their swords into plowshares, and their spears into pruning-
hooks: nation shall not lift up sword against nation, neither shall
they learn war any more" (Is 2:4; Mic 4:3). But this is predicated
on the rule of Christ over the earth: "He shall judge among the
nations." Psalm 72:7 adds, "In his days shall the righteous flour-
ish; and abundance of peace so long as the moon endureth." But
men lost the immediate prospect of peace when they murdered
the Prince of peace and said, "Away with him, crucify him."
They said, "We have no king but Caesar," and it has been Caesar
ever since. They said, "Not this man, but Barabbas." Scripture
says Barabbas was a murderer, so man is getting what he chose.

**23   What are some of the other conditions predicted to come on the
earth besides universal peace?**

One will be the removal of the curse which God put upon
the ground because of man's sin (Gen 3:17-19). It is this which
caused the ground to bring forth thorns and thistles, and this is
why weeds are so prolific. In that day, "instead of the thorn shall
come up the fir tree, and instead of the brier shall come up the
myrtle tree: and it shall be to the LORD for a name, for an everlasting sign that shall not be cut off" (Is 55:13). This will make
it easy for all men to make a living. "Then shall the earth yield
her increase; and God, even our own God, shall bless us. God
shall bless us; and all the ends of the earth shall fear him" (Ps
67:6-7). This will result in such fruitfulness as the world has
never known. "Behold, the days come, saith the LORD, that the
plowman shall overtake the reaper, and the treader of grapes him
that soweth seed; and the mountains shall drop sweet wine"
(Amos 9:13).

This condition will be accompanied by a change in the animal
world. "The wolf also shall dwell with the lamb, and the leopard
shall lie down with the kid; and the calf and the young lion and

the fatling together; and a little child shall lead them. And the cow and the bear shall feed; their young ones shall lie down together: and the lion shall eat straw like the ox" (Is 11:6-7). The prophet goes on: "And the sucking child shall play on the hole of the asp, and the weaned child shall put his hand on the cockatrice' den. They shall not hurt nor destroy in all my holy mountain: for the earth shall be full of the knowledge of the LORD, as the waters cover the sea." All of this goes far beyond anything men have ever dreamed of.

How will man share in these conditions?   24

Special blessings are promised to him too. It appears that the span of life will be increased to a thousand years, so that none will die in infancy, and no one will become decrepit. "There shall be no more thence an infant of days, nor an old man that hath not filled his days" (Is 65:20). The poor will no longer be exploited by the rich. "They shall build houses, and inhabit them; and they shall plant vineyards, and eat the fruit of them. They shall not build, and another inhabit; they shall not plant, and another eat: for as the days of a tree are the days of my people, and mine elect shall long enjoy the work of their hands," the passage goes on to say.

What about those who do sin or cause trouble?   25

Such persons will be dealt with promptly. Psalm 101:8 says, "Morning by morning I will destroy the wicked out of the land" (ASV). "With righteousness shall he judge the poor, and reprove with equity for the meek of the earth: and he shall smite the earth with the rod of his mouth, and with the breath of his lips shall he slay the wicked" (Is 11:4). There will be no laxity in the administration of justice. If a person commits sin, he has until the following morning to get right with God. Otherwise there will be the extreme penalty of death, as in the early days of Israel (Num 15:30-36). Satan will be bound for the thousand years (Rev 20:1-3), and in the absence of outward pressures, any sin will be presumptuous.

26   Why doesn't God bring in these conditions now?

All of God's acts are timed in keeping with His eternal counsels. These include both His dealings with individuals and with
all humanity. He is the God of the infinite and of the infinitesimal,
the God of time and of eternity. If He delays dealing with nations, we can be sure it will be as with Christ's first advent:
"When the fullness of the time was come, God sent forth his
Son." In the meantime He is concerned with all that concerns
us; and when His time comes, He acts. Frequently during His
lifetime the Lord Jesus said, "My time is not yet come." Finally
He said, "The hour is come." His actions were governed strictly
by God's timing for Him. At God's appointed time His Son will
come the second time, and the prophecies concerning that coming
will all be fulfilled as literally as were those of His first advent,
now so many years ago.

SALVATION

What Does It Mean to Be Born Again?

What did Jesus mean when He said, "Ye must be born again"?   27

The new birth is the impartation of eternal life to those who believe in Christ and acknowledge Him as their personal Saviour. Eternal life is God's own life which, when imparted to us, makes us the children of God. This is not simply a title. We are made alive spiritually with the divine life and nature (Jn 3:36; 2 Pe 1:4). The new birth is an integral part of salvation, and without it no one can be saved. The Lord Jesus said, "Verily, verily, I say unto thee, Except a man be born again, he cannot see the kingdom of God" (Jn 3:3).

The penalty for sin consists of two parts, death and judgment. "It is appointed unto men once to die, but after this the judgment" (Heb 9:27). The Lord Jesus bore God's judgment against sin when He hung on the cross. Then He entered into the experience of death and overcame its power in resurrection. This is why His resurrection is stressed so in the Bible. "Because I live, ye shall live also," He promised (Jn 14:19). We are not simply forgiven sinners, which would have been our status had Christ only borne the judgment of God against sin. We are now children of God, because we are made partakers of His divine, eternal life. This gives us a status higher than that of Adam before he sinned.

How is this new birth accomplished?   28

It is an act of the Holy Spirit. "That which is born of the flesh is flesh; and that which is born of the Spirit is spirit" (Jn 3:6). The agency used is the Word of God. "Being born again, not of corruptible seed, but of incorruptible, by the word of God, which liveth and abideth for ever" (1 Pe 1:23). And so that there may be no doubt about this, Peter adds in verse 25: "The word of the Lord endureth for ever. And this is the word which by the gospel is preached unto you." Hence it is clear that the gospel is "the power of God unto salvation to everyone that believeth" (Ro 1:16).

29 Some hold that the new birth is effected by baptism. Is there any biblical basis for this?

The text usually referred to in this connection is John 3:5: "Jesus answered, Verily, verily, I say unto thee, Except a man be born of water and of the Spirit, he cannot enter into the kingdom of God." If the water refers to baptism, which many question, it would be John's baptism that is in view, for Christian baptism was not yet instituted. John said, "I indeed baptize you with water unto repentance: but he that cometh after me is mightier than I, whose shoes I am not worthy to bear: he shall baptize you with the Holy Ghost, and with fire" (Mt 3:11). If John 3:5 refers to baptism it would mean that besides the repentance symbolized in John's baptism, we also need the baptism of the Spirit to become children of God. Paul wrote in 1 Corinthians 12:13: "By one Spirit are we all baptized into one body . . . and have been all made to drink into one Spirit." Besides repentance we need the life-giving action of the Holy Spirit, in response to our faith in Christ.

30 How do those explain John 3:5 who do not take it to refer to baptism?

A commonly held view is that the water is symbolic of the Word of God, which Peter declares is the agency by which we are born again. Elsewhere in the Bible water is used as a symbol of Scripture, as in Ephesians 5:26, where, after we are told that Christ loved the Church and gave Himself for it, it is added: "That he might sanctify and cleanse it with the washing of water by the word." This accords with what is said in Titus 3:5: "Not by works of righteousness which we have done, but according to his mercy he saved us, by the washing of regeneration, and renewing of the Holy Ghost."

Some object to this interpretation of John 3:5 on the ground that it mixes a metaphor, *water*, with a literal term, *the Spirit*. This has been countered with the suggestion that the verse can be translated: "Except a man be born of water and wind," making both terms figurative. While water is used as a symbol of the Word of God, wind is used as a symbol of the Holy Spirit, as in Acts 2:2. Whatever interpretation we adopt, the resulting sense is the same, that there must be repentance and faith on our part, and a work of the Holy Spirit imparting eternal life to us.

What steps must a person take to experience this new birth?   31

We have what might almost be called a formula for this in John 1:12-13: "As many as received him, to them gave he power to become the sons [children] of God, even to them that believe on his name: Which were born, not of blood, nor of the will of the flesh, nor of the will of man, but of God." Verse 11 tells us that when He came to His own, His own received Him not. Then we are assured that those who did receive Him were given the right to become God's children. *Receiving* Him is defined as "believing on His name." This is not meant to be mysterious, but rather to be understood by anyone who desires to enter into this experience.

For those having difficulty in understanding what it means to receive Christ, perhaps the illustration of marriage will help, especially since that very figure is used in the Bible of our relationship to Christ. After a prospective bride and groom express their desire to marry and have received the legal authorization required, each is asked if he takes the other as husband or wife. Upon their declaration before witnesses that they do, they are pronounced man and wife. It is not a matter of how they feel. And sometimes in the early hours of marriage they may be self-conscious about the relationship because they do not yet *feel* married; but they *are* married. And if a Christian questions whether the Lord Jesus has actually received him, he can be assured by Christ's own statement: "Him that cometh to me I will in no wise cast out" (Jn 6:37). No one has ever sincerely said "yes" to Christ and then had Christ say "no" to him. If we come to Him acknowledging our sins and confess Him as our personal Lord and Saviour, He promises to confess us before His Father in heaven (Mt 10:32), and we can know, on the firm assurance of God's Word, that we are brought into the family of God.

Can We Be Sure of Heaven?

32 Is it possible to know with certainty that we will go to heaven when we die?

Such assurance is not only possible, it is the basis of fruitful Christian living. It is when we know for certain that we are children of God by faith in Jesus Christ that we can order our lives by the will of God as revealed in His Word. The various New Testament writers not only asserted such assurance concerning themselves but also taught that others could have the same assurance. It is both possible and highly desirable to be thus assured.

33 Can you give examples of some expressions of this assurance?

In 1 Corinthians 1:18 the apostle Paul refers to those who are perishing and in contrast speaks of "us which are saved." He not only indicates that there is such a category, he includes himself in it. In 2 Corinthians 4:3 he mentions "them that are lost," dissociating himself from that group. The apostle Peter, addressing the household of Cornelius, the Roman centurion, assured them that "to him [Christ] give all the prophets witness, that through his name whosoever believeth in him shall receive remission of sins" (Ac 10:43). Peter's epistles, addressed to believers in Christ, declare that they have been redeemed and born again (1 Pe 1:18-23). He makes it clear that the "hope" of salvation does not mean the hope of becoming saved but the hope or outlook which accompanies salvation (1 Pe 1:3-5). Hope here implies assurance of acceptance with God.

The apostle John is very explicit. He declares that his Gospel was written "that ye might believe that Jesus is the Christ, the

Son of God; and that believing ye might have life through his name" (Jn 20:31). He later wrote: "These things I am writing to you that you may *know* that you have eternal life—you who believe in the name of the Son of God" (1 Jn 5:13, Confraternity Revision—italics ours). This emphatically teaches that believers in Christ are intended to have the assurance of salvation.

On what ground is this possible?   34

There are two aspects to this question. The first is What does God require for the expiation of sin? The other is What does He demand of us for this to become effective in us? "The wages of sin is death" (Ro 6:23), and Christ's death on our behalf makes possible the balance of that verse: "but the gift of God is eternal life through Jesus Christ our Lord." The holiness of God demands the payment of the penalty for sin. "Without shedding of blood is no remission" (Heb 9:22). This refers back to the Jewish ritual, but this ritual was instituted to show the necessity for Christ's atonement, and so the text has validity and relevance for us. Sin is forgiven because it was judged in the person of Christ on the cross. It is only as we are in Him, by faith, that we can be acceptable to God.

On our part God demands repentance and faith (Ac 17:30-31; 16:31). The constant call of the gospel is to "whosoever believeth" (Jn 3:16). While repentance and faith are not identical, they are inseparable on the part of fallen, sinful humanity. A man could not have faith in the living God without the consciousness of sin; and he could not have the God-given consciousness of sin, wrought by the Holy Spirit, without seeking the mercy of God through acceptance of the gospel message. When one has repentance and faith, God imparts eternal life to that one and he is born again (Jn 1:12-13). This gives him the right to be called a child of God. The common concept that all men are "children of God" is thus shown to be fallacious. Man is a creature of God, originally made in God's image, but this image has been marred. Even before the advent of sin into human experience, however, man did not possess the eternal life of God. He had creature life. But in redemption we are made partakers of the eternal life of God and of His divine nature (Jn 3:16; 2 Pe 1:4). It is on this ground that we have acceptance with God.

35   How can a person be sure he is accepted with God?

It has been said that "the blood of Christ makes us safe; the
Word of God makes us sure." We see in many passages of Scripture that God must judge sin. Mercy and grace do not imply
overlooking sin, as many persons seem to think. It is rather that
because God is merciful, He sent His only begotten Son to become our Saviour by taking our place in the judgment. When
men showed their hatred of God by rejecting His Son (Mt 21:33-
39), God used the occasion of His crucifixion to lay our sins on
Him. "The Lord hath laid on him the iniquity of us all" (Is
53:6). Christ's death might, in one sense, be considered to be that
of a martyr, but it was far more than that. The apostle Peter
wrote: "Christ also hath once suffered for sins, the just for the unjust, that he might bring us to God, being put to death in the
flesh, but quickened by the Spirit" (1 Pe 3:18). He "gave himself a ransom for all, to be testified in due time" (1 Ti 2:6).

The Bible assures us in many passages that because of Christ's
atonement, the sins of those who trust in Him are put away. He
"put away sin by the sacrifice of himself" (Heb 9:26). Consequently the promise is: "Their sins and iniquities will I remember
no more" (Heb 10:17). Had sin only been overlooked there
would be no assurance that the question would not arise again in
the future. As the matter stands we are reckoned to be "dead
indeed unto sin, but alive unto God through Jesus Christ our
Lord" (Ro 6:11).

**36   Does God give a sign of some kind when we are accepted by
Him?**

While many persons do experience some special manifestation
of the Holy Spirit in connection with their salvation, none is required for us to have the assurance that we are saved. Many experience a special joy in God, the influx of spiritual power, and an
immediate change in their outlook. They have new desires and
often discard old ones. But not everyone has the same experience,
and with many, changes come about gradually. To rest on some
experience of this kind would leave us open to doubts ever after.
When we accept what God says, He fulfills His pledges regardless
of how we feel. And God's Word never changes. We can always

point to Scripture and say, "God says it, and I believe it." This gives assurance that will never fail.

Can Salvation Be Lost?

If a person is once truly saved, can he later be lost again?   37

This question presents a problem, whatever answer is given. If we hold that someone can be saved and later lost, we rob believers of their assurance of salvation. Many live in constant fear that they may do something (or perhaps feel that they have already done something) which will nullify the salvation they obtained by trusting in Christ. Others feel that if we believe a person once truly saved can never be lost, we open the door to licentiousness. For those holding this view the doctrine sometimes referred to as "the security of the believer" is an abomination to be shunned. It has even been called "a doctrine of the devil."

However doctrines are not derived by considering what may be their consequences. We arrive at our doctrinal beliefs on the basis of what the Bible teaches, and then we leave the matter of consequences with God, in the realization that whatever God reveals as truth will produce the right consequences. In our understanding of the Bible, we believe that a person once truly saved will not later be lost. We base this, not only on so-called proof texts, but on a number of other considerations as well. Those who reject this teaching also have what they consider proof texts. We believe that such "proofs" for either view should be weighed in the light of all that the Bible teaches on the subject.

What are some of the proofs that a person once saved can never 38
be lost?

A familiar one is the Lord Jesus' statement in John 10:27-30: "My sheep hear my voice, and I know them, and they follow me: and I give unto them eternal life; and they shall never perish, neither shall any man pluck them out of my hand. My Father, which gave them me, is greater than all; and no man is able to pluck them out of my Father's hand. I and my Father are one."

The word "man" is not in the text, which should read: ". . . no one is able to pluck them out of my Father's hand." This would include any demon or even Satan himself. We consider it a specious argument, of no weight, to say that a person could pluck *himself* out of the Father's hand. The picture is rather that of security by the combined strength of the Father and the Son.

Other texts assert that the believer in Christ has "everlasting life" (Jn 3:36) and that his sins and iniquities will not be remembered against him (Heb 10:17). John 5:24 states that he will not even come into "condemnation," or judgment, which is considered a better rendering. He is "accepted in the beloved" (Eph 1:6) and is made to sit "in heavenly places in Christ Jesus" (Eph 2:6). There are many similar statements in the Bible which show that salvation is a completed work in the present time.

39   **You mentioned proof texts for the view that a saved person can become lost: what are some of these?**

Perhaps the most familiar are two similar passages in the epistle to the Hebrews. In 6:4-6 we read: "It is impossible for those who were once enlightened, and have tasted of the heavenly gift, and were made partakers of the Holy Ghost, and have tasted the good word of God, and the powers of the world to come, if they shall fall away, to renew them again unto repentance; seeing they crucify to themselves the Son of God afresh, and put him to an open shame." A somewhat similar passage is in 10:26-29. Both passages speak of a deliberate rejection of Christ, with a full understanding of the issues involved.

The question is whether these passages describe a saved person who becomes lost or whether they are showing how far a person can advance in spiritual enlightenment without actually being born again. Our view of the passage will be determined by what we consider to be the teaching of the entire Bible on the subject. A third alternative, held by many, is that the passage does not refer to eternal salvation but to the fruitfulness of a believer. Those holding this view consider that certain sins not only limit a believer's usefulness temporarily but can render him incapable of restoration to a life of fruitful communion with God. We cannot now discuss this, but I do not believe it represents the intended sense of the passage.

What are some of the other truths which have a bearing on our   40
interpretation of these particular texts?

One is the consideration of all that goes into salvation. When we consider all that was involved in God's gift of His Son to become our Saviour and then the divine transaction which takes place when we by faith receive Christ as our Saviour, it seems incongruent to make salvation a fluctuating experience of such nature that we may have it one day and lose it the next, and then perhaps recapture it the third day. This would not only give Christ's atonement temporary (instead of eternal) value, but it would also mean a limited atonement, so that if we once had the experience of being lost after having been saved, recovery would be forever impossible.

Why would recovery be impossible?   41

If a person were trusting in the atoning blood of Christ and were saved, and then later committed a sin (any sin) which caused him to become lost, it would be evidence that that sin was not covered by the atonement. Consequently there would not be any ground on which it could be forgiven subsequently. To be lost after having been saved would mean a reversal of all that was done when we became saved. Our sins which were forgiven, and which God promised not to remember (Heb 10:17), would have to be charged against us again. At conversion we were taken out of Adam and put into Christ (Ro 5-6). We should now have to be taken out of Christ and put back in Adam. Since we are seated "together in heavenly places in Christ Jesus" (Eph 2:6), this also would have to be nullified. But worst of all, it would be saying that Christ's atonement did not cover all our sins. Had that been true, we never would have been saved at all, for salvation, to be effective, must put away all, or every, sin. In 1 John 1:7 we are assured that this is exactly what the blood of Christ does for the believer.

Is It Possible for a Person to Be Mistaken with Regard to Salvation?

42   Does the Bible say that some people think they are saved, when actually they are not?

Yes, this is clearly the case. Paul wrote to the Corinthian church about some of its members who professed conversion to Christ but who continued to live in sin. He indicated that their profession of faith in Christ could be considered to be spurious if there was no resulting change in their way of life. Newness of life in Christ produces fruits worthy of God and of the Christian faith. There are other forms of self-deception too. Some trust in outward religious ceremony without ever having had an actual encounter with Christ. They have not recognized themselves to be lost and acknowledged Him as their Lord and Saviour on the ground of His substitutionary death on their behalf. Still others, instead of relying on what Christ has done for them on the cross, rely on what they think they are doing for God, assuming this will win them acceptance with Him. Some depend on their own sufferings in this life to expiate their sins. A statement often heard is: "I've had my hell here on earth." Such a thought has no biblical basis whatever.

43   How does Scripture deal with these ideas?

The Lord Jesus exposes the falsity of them. In Luke 13:23-28 we read of some who think they are bona fide members of Christ's kingdom but who are rejected by Him. A study of the text indicates that they have trusted in things comparable to church attendance, and perhaps the partaking of the Lord's Supper. "We have eaten and drunk in thy presence, and thou hast taught in our streets," they plead. Yet the Lord answers, "I know you not whence ye are; depart from me, all ye workers of iniquity." If they had been in such close contact with Him, they should have known Him in a vital way. It is evident that they have been satisfied with a superficial acknowledgment of Christ and Chris-

tianity and have never submitted their lives to Him in the obedience of faith. They have not been born again. The Lord Jesus
Himself said, "Verily, verily, I say unto thee, Except a man be
born again, he cannot see the kingdom of God" (Jn 3:3).

What about those who trust in their works?   44

Matthew 7:21-29 contains a passage somewhat parallel to that
in Luke 13. Those speaking here seem to have placed confidence
in their own good works: "Lord, have we not prophesied in thy
name? and in thy name have cast out devils? and in thy name
done many wonderful works?" Yet the Lord replies, "I never
knew you: depart from me, ye that work iniquity." Here the re-
vealing phrase is: "I never knew you." It is not that they had
once been saved but now are lost: Christ never knew them.

Such a passage need not unsettle the faith of a true believer.
Referred to here are those who, instead of coming to Christ first
for salvation and then offering themselves to Him for His service,
had assumed they could find acceptance with God through what
they could do for Him. Scripture makes it clear that we become
saved on the ground of what Christ did for us on the cross. Many
scriptures show that our works in no way procure God's favor.
One such passage is Ephesians 2:8-9, where we read: "By grace
are ye saved through faith; and that not of yourselves: it is the
gift of God: not of works, lest any man should boast."

Does what we endure in this life in the way of suffering have any   45
bearing on our salvation?

None whatever. We are saved or lost according to whether or
not we are "in Christ" by faith in Him. Sin is not put away by
suffering—not even the suffering of Christ, apart from His death
and resurrection. "The wages of sin is death," we read in Romans
6:23, and nothing short of death would give God ground to forgive sins. While 1 Peter 3:18 says, "Christ also hath once suffered
for sins, the just for the unjust, that he might bring us to God,"
the apostle immediately adds: "being put to death in the flesh,
but quickened by the Spirit." Romans 4:25 says of Christ: "Who
was delivered for our offenses, and was raised again for our justifi-

cation." It is only by the blood of His atonement that sin is purged (Ro 3:25).

Further, if any sufferings of ours entered into the basis of our acceptance with God it would rob Christ of His unique glory in becoming our Saviour. Hebrews 1:3 says of Him: "Who being the brightness of his glory, and the express image of his person, and upholding all things by the word of his power, when he had by himself purged our sins, sat down on the right hand of the Majesty on high." It was "by himself" he purged our sins, and no one can share that glory. Had Christ's death not been an absolute necessity for our redemption, we can be sure God would not have caused Him to go through that experience. In fact, our Lord's thrice-repeated prayer in Gethsemane makes it crystal clear that there was no other way whereby we could be saved.

46   What about those who profess Christianity but continue to sin?

Such a situation raises serious question as to the validity of one's profession. The apostle Paul wrote the Corinthians about that very subject, and after remonstrating with them about some of the things they were doing, he said, "Know ye not that the unrighteous shall not inherit the kingdom of God? Be not deceived: neither fornicators, nor idolaters, nor adulterers, nor effeminate, nor abusers of themselves with mankind, nor thieves, nor covetous, nor drunkards, nor revilers, nor extortioners, shall inherit the kingdom of God." And to show the change which the experience of salvation brings, he added: "And such were some of you: but ye are washed, but ye are sanctified, but ye are justified in the name of the Lord Jesus, and by the Spirit of our God" (1 Co 6:9-11).

It is true that a child of God may fall into sin, but when one can contemplate such a situation with complacency and consider that his profession of faith will keep him from the consequences of his sin, it raises the suspicion that his profession of faith is not genuine. Only God knows with certainty, and He is the judge to whom we must give our account; but it behooves each of us to make sure that he is not deceiving himself.

Are Some Persons Predestined to Be Lost?

We often hear it said that certain persons are predestined to be 47
saved; does this mean that others are predestined to be lost?

In my understanding of the Bible no one is predestinated either
to be saved or lost. The term occurs some six times in the New
Testament. One use is somewhat abstract in Ephesians 1:11. In
the other passages the term refers to certain things which God
determined in advance, for example, in Ephesians 1:5, the position of sons to which God predestined believers in this dispensation. This verse is in accord with Romans 8:29, but the term is
not used to indicate that God, acting in His sovereign right, predetermined either the salvation or judgment of anyone. In Acts
4:28 we are told that God predetermined the death of His Son in
order that He might become the Saviour of those who trust in
Him. We therefore do not believe that people are predestinated
to be saved or lost.

If the Bible does not state that people are predestined to be saved 48
or lost, how did this idea originate?

The idea probably grew out of a confusion of terms. While it
is not said that God predestined people to be saved or lost, Scripture does say that some are *elected* to be saved. Many have assumed that election is equivalent to predetermination. However,
the doctrine of election is explained in 1 Peter 1:2 as being based
on God's foreknowledge. Hence God does not arbitrarily elect
some to be saved, omitting others. We are told, both positively
and negatively, that as far as God's will is concerned He desires
the salvation of all men (1 Ti 2:3-4), and is not willing that any
should perish (1 Pe 3:9). If the choice were made on the basis of
God's desire He would have chosen all. Ezekiel 33:11 and other
passages confirm this truth. Any limitation of God on the number
of those benefiting by Christ's redemption is not made on the basis
of God's reluctance to save all men, but rather, as stated elsewhere in Scripture, because men do not fulfill the requirements
God has laid down, in keeping with His holiness and other attributes.

49   What are the requirements for anyone to become saved?

Acts 17:30-31 makes it clear that one requirement is to come to God in a spirit of repentance: "God . . . now commandeth all men every where to repent: because he hath appointed a day in which he will judge the world in righteousness by that man whom he hath ordained; whereof he hath given assurance unto all men, in that he hath raised him from the dead." This prophecy may have reference to the judgments of God on the world during the coming tribulation period, but the commandment applies *now*, and has universal force—all men, everywhere.

The other requirement mentioned throughout the New Testament is that we believe on the Lord Jesus Christ, God's Son whom He has sent to be the Saviour of the world. "He that believeth on the Son hath everlasting life: and he that believeth not the Son shall not see life; but the wrath of God abideth on him" (Jn 3:36). "Believe on the Lord Jesus Christ and thou shalt be saved, and thy house" (Ac 16:31). Again, "Be it known unto you therefore, men and brethren, that through this man is preached unto you the forgiveness of sins: and by him all that believe are justified from all things, from which ye could not be justified by the law of Moses" (Ac 13:38-39). One could multiply such references. These are the two conditions: on the negative side, we acknowledge our lost and sinful condition; on the positive side we receive and acknowledge Jesus Christ as our Lord and Saviour, through faith in Him. Because these are the terms, God will not save those who fail to meet them.

50   Does this mean that man determines his own destiny?

In the sense of responsibility, yes, though the entire thrust to save men comes from God. It was He who sought men, not the reverse. God desired that man should be saved and devised the plan to make it possible (2 Sa 14:14). But man is not saved by a plan; he is saved through the Person and work of Christ. Had not God provided the Person to carry out the plan, man could not have been saved even had he desired it. And not only has God designed the plan and brought it to accomplishment, He has sent the Holy Spirit into the world to bring conviction to men (Jn 16:7-15), and He has commissioned those who believe in

Christ to go into all the world and preach the gospel to every creature (Mk 16:15). In this respect, salvation is all of God. But He has made its effectiveness dependent on man's acceptance of Christ, and the acknowledgment of his own lost condition. In that sense each person is accountable to God. If he becomes saved, he can rightly say that salvation is all of God, since all was provided for him, and he was invited and urged to accept it. If he remains in his sins, he has no one to blame but himself.

Does not this requirement of faith in Christ give man something to boast about in becoming saved? 51

This claim is often made but Scripture expressly denies the validity of this statement. In Romans 3:27 Paul wrote: "Where is boasting then? It is excluded. By what law? of works? Nay: but by the law of faith." That is to say, the law of faith excludes boasting. This verse is a plain declaration that the exercise of faith in receiving Christ as Saviour cannot be considered a work of merit. The very terms of the gospel exclude any boasting on the part of the one who receives God's gift of eternal life through faith in Christ.

Calvin has an enlightening comment on this subject in his commentary on Galatians: "For this righteousness is not a quality which exists in men, but is the mere gift of God, and is enjoyed by faith only; and not even as a reward justly due to faith, but because we receive by faith what God freely gives. All such expressions as the following are of similar import: We are 'justified freely by his grace' (Ro 3:24). Christ is our righteousness. The mercy of God is the cause of our righteousness. By the death and resurrection of Christ, righteousness has been procured for us. Righteousness is bestowed on us through the gospel. We obtain righteousness by faith." But while the exercise of faith in Christ is not an act of merit, it is necessary if we are to become saved. So let us each ask ourselves, "Have I personally received Jesus Christ as my Lord and Saviour, and do I acknowledge Him in word and act in my daily life?" "Trust in the Lord with all thine heart; and lean not unto thine own understanding. In all thy ways acknowledge him, and he shall direct thy paths" (Pr 3:5-6).

Did Christ Die for Everyone, or Only for a Limited Number of Persons?

52 Was the atonement of Christ intended to be universal in its extent, or was it limited to certain persons foreknown by God or predestinated to be saved?

This question has been a subject of much debate between different schools of thought. Almost everyone admits that in *some* sense Christ died for everyone, though there are those who teach that His death was not available to all as an atonement for sin. Some adopt the formula that Christ was a propitiation for the whole world (1 Jn 2:2), but that He was a substitute only for those who would believe on Him. "This is my blood of the new testament [or 'covenant'], which is shed for many for the remission of sins" (Mt 26:28). Certain Bible students take this and other references to "many" to mean that He did not bear the sins of all. Others argue that the "many" is in contrast with the "One" who bore the sins and that it is not intended to limit the extent of Christ's atonement.

53 Does the view of limited atonement restrict the preaching of the gospel?

Not necessarily, though some who have adopted this view consider that the preaching of the gospel is not needed. They believe that whoever is to be saved will be saved, by whatever means God decides to use. Hence we have only to live the Christian life and to witness as the Lord enables, but without special concern about whether others believe or not. We cannot persuade those who are not of "the elect," and the others are sure to become saved in God's good time. But this attitude is not inherent in the idea of limited atonement, and some argue that since God alone knows who will be saved, we should witness to all to the extent of our ability and opportunity to do so, even though only those predestined to eternal life can actually become saved.

Are there any "proof texts" for either of these views?   54

Yes, for both. Those who hold the view of *unlimited* atonement
refer to texts which speak of Christ dying for the entire world,
e.g., "The Father sent the Son to be the Saviour of the world"
(1 Jn 4:14). They also point to the universality of the invitation
to believe and be saved—"Whosoever will, let him take the water
of life freely" (Rev 22:17). John 3:16 combines these statements:
"For God so loved the world, that he gave his only begotten Son,
that whosoever believeth in him should not perish, but have everlasting life." On the other side reference is made to such texts as:
"It is not of him that willeth, nor of him that runneth, but of God
that showeth mercy. Therefore hath he mercy on whom he will
have mercy, and whom he will be hardeneth" (Ro 9:16, 18).
There are other texts also which are thought by some to teach that
certain people cannot be saved.

Is there any way to reconcile these views?   55

I do not believe the two views can be reconciled, because they
are opposites, but all of the scriptures involved can be reconciled
into a single interpretation. However, as in all cases of disagree-
ment, each person follows what seems to him the most logical
interpretation, consonant with all that the Bible teaches on the
subject. But I would reject the idea that God's sovereignty and
man's responsibility are mutually contradictory. Unfortunately
schools of thought have become established, and often one argues
for the one of his preference. This tends to arouse patriotism for
the view we adopt, rather than objective consideration of all that
is involved. We put people into categories and then interpret
what they say on the basis of the supposed views of those in that
category.

How would you explain the teaching of Scripture in regard to   56
this question?

In my understanding of the subject the atonement is not limited, but it is conditional. That is to say, the value of Christ's
death is more than sufficient for the salvation of all mankind; and
it is available to all, if they will receive it. But God has made
salvation conditional on its being received by faith. Those who

do not make this response are not benefitted by Christ's sacrifice. Rather, its being provided and rejected, or neglected, adds to their condemnation. The fact that God foreknows what the decision will be, and so is prepared to deal appropriately, does not mean that He has Himself made the determination. God "will have all men to be saved" (1 Ti 2:4) and is "not willing that any should perish" (2 Pe 3:9). If it were left to Him, everyone would be saved. But in His sovereignty, God has decreed that we must believe in order to be saved, and 1 Peter 1:2 informs us that God made His choice on the basis of His foreknowledge. For God to make the decision and then hold man accountable for that decision seems to me to contradict all that the Bible tells us of the character of God.

57   If man is required to believe the gospel in order to be saved, can this be considered a "good work" on his part?

No, although this is often claimed. But Scripture anticipates this and denies it. Romans 3:27 says, "Where is boasting then? It is excluded. By what law? of works? Nay: but by the law of faith." That is to say, the fact that salvation is obtained through faith does not make it a good work in which one can boast. Calvin says, in his commentary on Galatians, "Not even as a reward justly due to faith, but because we receive by faith what God freely gives." Some have thought that Ephesians 2:8-9 proves that faith is imparted to some as a special gift of God. But we believe this is erroneous. The text reads: "For by grace are ye saved through faith: and that not of yourselves: it is the gift of God: not of works, lest any man should boast." The last clause shows that it is salvation which is still in view. This is confirmed by the fact that in the original language both "grace" and "faith" are feminine, while the demonstrative "that" is neuter and so could not refer to either of these. A. T. Robertson says in his *Word Pictures in the New Testament*, " 'Grace' is God's part, 'faith' ours. *And that* (*kai touto*). Neuter, not feminine *taute*, and so refers not to *pistis* (feminine) or to *charis* (feminine also), but to the act of being saved by grace conditioned on faith on our part. Paul shows that salvation does not have its source (*ex humon*, out of you) in men, but from God. Besides, it is God's gift (*doron*) and not the result of our work." All of this seems to me to confirm that Christ's atonement was infinite in scope, because He who made it was infinite, being God. Its limitation to those who believe is not due to limited value of the atonement, but to the fact that it is offered to man on the condition that he receive it in faith. It becomes effective in all who believe but confers no benefit on the unbeliever.

What Is an Apostate?

Is the term "apostate" biblical? What does it mean?   **58**

No person in the Bible is described by the term apostate, but the act of apostasy is mentioned twice in the Greek text. In Acts 21:21 we read that the elders in Jerusalem relayed to Paul certain accusations currently being made against him. One of these was that he taught the Jews who lived in predominantly Gentile areas that they should "forsake Moses," having reference to the rite of circumcision and other customs of the Jews. It is literally that he was teaching "apostasy from Moses." What he actually taught was that believers in Christ are not under law, but under grace (Ro 6:14). The word *apostasy* means the abandonment of what one has voluntarily professed; the total desertion of principles or faith. The other passage where the word is used is 2 Thessalonians 2:3 where we read, "For that day shall not come, except there come a falling away first." The Greek text has the definite article, and reads, "except there be the apostasy first." A cognate word is used for divorce, and this again gives the thought of abandonment of a previously professed devotion.

Since the word "apostate" is not used of anyone in the Bible, does   **59**
this mean no one in Bible times had that character?

By no means, for while the word apostate is not used, the idea is expressed in more than one passage. However, since the terms apostasy and apostate are not defined in the Bible, our understanding of them must be determined by the theological truth and circumstances involved. There are those who consider that one may be a true Christian in the biblical sense of having had a personal conversion to Christ, of having been born again in the power of the Holy Spirit, and yet fall away and become an apostate. As we have explained elsewhere, we do not believe this to be possible. Rather, we take it that an apostate is one who has professed Christianity, with understanding of what is involved, yet has not had the inward commitment to Christ which results in the new birth. It is more in the nature of a mental commitment. Such a person may, through various pressures, be induced to give up his profession. It may be on account of persecution due to one's being a professed Christian, or it may be caused by a sense of shame in the presence of those who hold Christianity in contempt. Sometimes a person by intellectual pursuit comes to the conviction that Christianity is intellectually untenable. Such persons themselves often hold Christianity in contempt in later life, and have been known to oppose vigorously the preaching of Christianity.

60 What are some of the Bible passages which speak of such an experience?

One is found in the parables of the Lord Jesus. The first of the seven parables found in Matthew 13 describes four different conditions which parallel different states of soul on the part of those who hear the Word of God. The first is like seed falling on a footpath, which cannot become rooted, and the birds eat it up. The second illustrates the truth of which we are speaking. It springs up but, when the heat of the sun beats upon it, it dies. The Lord explains that because there was no depth of earth the seed had not actually rooted itself. Luke 8:13 says, "And these have no root, which for a while believe, and in time of temptation fall away." There are signs of life, but it is clearly stated in each of the gospels in which this parable is recorded that the seed, in this instance, was never rooted.

61 Do other New Testament writers speak of this condition?

Yes. It is described in detail in several passages of Scripture. In 2 Peter 2:17-22 we read of some who "have escaped the pol-

lutions of the world through the knowledge of the Lord and
Saviour Jesus Christ," but who are "again entangled therein, and
overcome." It is said of these that "the latter end is worse with
them than the beginning. For it had been better for them not to
have known the way of righteousness, than, after they have
known it, to turn from the holy commandment delivered unto
them." We might well suppose that these had once been saved,
but verse 22 says, "It is happened unto them according to the
true proverb, The dog is turned to his own vomit again; and the
sow that was washed to her wallowing in the mire." This shows
clearly that there had not been any change of basic nature. The
dog remained a dog throughout. He became sick of his former
state and vomited out what troubled him. Later he returned to
the very thing he had discarded. Likewise the sow was washed
but not changed, and she finally returned to her former state. The
person symbolized had experienced an outward change of life
due to spiritual enlightenment, but not an inward change of heart.
Such persons were never saved at all.

What are some other passages bearing on this subject?   62

The apostle John speaks of some who "went out from us, but
they were not of us" (1 Jn 2:19). Jude also speaks of some
who apparently were still active in the Christian community, but
whose life and teaching showed they had abandoned true Christianity. Paul in various places describes some who carried on
subversive work. Two passages in Hebrews refer to this subject.
Though scholars are not all in agreement as to the bearing of
Hebrews 6:4-6 and 10:26-31, we believe they parallel the passage
in 2 Peter 2. Chapter 6 of Hebrews shows how far a person can
go in Christian profession without being truly saved, and it reveals the judgment on those who abandon faith in Christ. Everything said in Hebrews 6:4-5, while normally describing faith in
Christ, can also be said in a limited sense of those who profess
Christianity without the reality of the new birth. Not only can
there be outward cleansing through enlightenment without inward change, as Peter shows, but men like Balaam and Judas experienced the working of the Holy Spirit in them. Balaam spoke
several messages by the Spirit of God, and there is every reason to

believe that Judas performed miracles similar to those of the other
eleven of the Lord's close disciples. Yet neither of these was ever
saved. We do not believe that Hebrews 6:6 applies to a believer.
We take the parables of verses 7 and 8 to show that one can be
subjected to the refreshing rain of heaven, and yet bring forth
thorns and briers.

The passage in Hebrews 10 is similar. The characteristic sin in
Hebrews is unbelief, and this seems indicated in verse 26. The
reference is not to the sins of the flesh committed in weakness,
but to a deliberate rejection of the Lord Jesus Christ and the
merits of His atoning blood. We believe the teaching of the entire New Testament shows that those who do this never experienced the change of heart which brings one into the new birth in
the power of the Holy Spirit. These two passages show, on the
other hand, that such deliberate rejection of Christ ensures the
final judgment of those who do so. This is quite different from a
believer who sins. When David was faced with judgment because
of a serious sin, he said, "Let us now fall into the hand of the
LORD; for his mercies are great" (2 Sa 24:14). He had recourse to
God in repentance. But for the apostate it is written: "It is a
fearful thing to fall into the hands of the living God" (Heb 10:31).

The Gospel and Social Work

63 **Is the term "social gospel" found in the Bible? If so, what does it
mean?**

The term is not found in the Bible. It is derived from the
ethical teaching of Christianity. Throughout the Bible we find
God expressing concern for the physical and material needs of
men. There are numerous instructions concerning the care of the
poor. Many of the beneficent works in the world had their origin
in Christian teaching. There were no public works of charity such
as hospitals, homes for orphans and old people, etc., in the ancient world, so far as we know. These are the outgrowth of the
application of biblical teaching to life. In this respect Christianity
has made an impact on the social life of the world, especially
where it has been adopted. Our Lord in His earthly life showed

great concern for the physical needs of men, especially among the poor (Lk 4:18-19).

Could this be considered the outworking of the golden rule, and hence the hallmark of Christianity? 64

The so-called "golden rule" is considered by many to be the epitome of the Christian faith, especially by those who do not recognize man's deeper and more critical need to be born again (Jn 3:3-7). But it is a significant factor in Christian living. Love of fellowmen (Lev 19:18) becomes an expression of the love of God to them. "Hereby perceive we the love of God, because he laid down his life for us: and we ought to lay down our lives for the brethren. But whoso hath this world's good [i.e., sustenance, what is necessary to life], and seeth his brother have need, and shutteth up his bowels of compassion from him, how dwelleth the love of God in him?" (1 Jn 3:16-17). The Christian faith does not ignore the physical and social needs of men. Some passages relate especially to the Christian community, but they go beyond this. Paul wrote: "As we have therefore opportunity, let us do good unto all men, especially unto them who are of the household of faith" (Gal 6:10).

Is not this the primary thrust of Christianity, and should not the meeting of man's material needs be given priority over preaching? 65

The late Theodore Roosevelt once asked this question of a missionary who worked among poor people. The missionary replied: "If the prodigal son had been supplied with money, food and clothing, how soon would he have returned to his father's house? Would he not have been likely to have stayed away?" The former President replied, "I see your point," and he had no further question. The Lord Jesus said, "A man's life consisteth not in the abundance of the things which he possesseth" (Lk 12:15). Again, "The life is more than meat, and the body is more than raiment" (v. 23). This is carried to its extreme in Matthew 10:28, where the Lord Jesus said, "Fear not them which kill the body, but are not able to kill the soul: but rather fear him which is able to destroy both soul and body in hell." Man's spiritual need is given complete priority over his physical need, even to the loss of life. There is the recognition of endless life which continues after the death of the body. "For what is a man profited, if he shall gain the whole world, and lose his own soul" (Mt 16:26). Spurgeon, the famed English preacher, said that anything given priority over salvation constitutes a bad bargain. He referred to Adam and Eve in Eden, and to Esau selling his birthright for a mess of pottage.

66   Could not this teaching be used as a means of encouraging the poor to accept their lot, while exonerating those who would exploit them?

Christianity does encourage the poor, but it in no wise excuses those who take advantage of them. Rather, it excoriates them. "Go to now, ye rich men, weep and howl for your miseries that shall come upon you" (Ja 5:1). God warns them that the rust of the things they have heaped up at the expense of the poor shall testify against them. The cavil that Christianity is a scheme to justify oppression of the poor is a lie propagated by the Communist Manifesto. It has been repeated so often that it is widely accepted today, even by many who have no sympathy for communist governments. But Christianity does supply a God-given comfort to the poor, and many have endured privation with Christian fortitude. The Bible teaches us that whatever we possess of material wealth is a stewardship, but many Christians suffer hardship where no human help is available. Receiving Christ as Saviour does not lead to a campaign against existing powers. Paul taught subjection to them (Ro 13), even though the emperor at that time was Nero, one of the worst tyrants of all history. It was he who condemned Paul to death.

The Lord Jesus said His kingdom was not of this world (Jn 18:36). He does not guarantee to change our circumstances, but He does change the inward state of those who trust in Him. As Christians we should seek the betterment of society. However, even when we succeed, if there has not been a corresponding spiritual gain, people are left in estrangement from God and face His judgment. We "were by nature the children of wrath, even as others" (Eph 2:3). "Except a man be born again, he cannot see the kingdom of God" (Jn 3:3). More important than any earthly

gain is the salvation of the soul. So great is the disparity in earthly
and heavenly values that Paul wrote: "Art thou called being a
servant [and the word is *slave*]? care not for it: but if thou mayest
be made free, use it rather" (1 Co 7:21). This had no reference
to the enslavement of black persons by whites; it was written at
a time when people were made slaves as the result of military
conquest. The slave might be a physician or other professional
man. Aesop, who wrote the philosophical fables, is said to have
been a slave. He lived about 600 B.C.

Does not this outlook favor the rich as against the poor or de-   67
prived?

On the contrary, it reduces human status to nothingness in the
light of eternity. One may be accounted great among men and be
nothing in the sight of God. The free man is Christ's servant; the
slave who becomes saved is the Lord's freed man (1 Co 7:22).
"Let the brother of low degree rejoice in that he is exalted: but
the rich, in that he is made low: because as the flower of the grass
he shall pass away" (Ja 1:9-10). Those in menial positions were
assured that they "serve the Lord Christ" (Col 3:22-24), and that
they would be rewarded by Him. But the whole thrust of the
Bible is that "we walk by faith, not by sight" (2 Co 5:7), and
that the issues of life are seen in eternity, rather than in this world.
It was the recognition of this which made men and women willing to die a martyr's death. Why make sacrifices at all if the true
values of life lie in the "here and now"? The martyrs were tri-
umphant in their confidence of an assured resurrection with the
Lord Jesus.

CHRISTIAN LIVING

Is Everything That Happens in the Will of God?

68 **With all the sorrow that is in the world, can we say that everything that happens is the will of God?**

In one sense we can say that nothing happens without God's permission, but this does not mean that God is complacent about its happening. Many think that if God is all-powerful, nothing can happen unless He designs and decrees it. But this overlooks certain important truths.

God could have made a universe in which nothing could happen except by His direction. In that case, the universe would be like a toy, with God manipulating all the controls. But there would be no companionship for God. Men and angels would be automatons, moving and acting as God designed and desired. But what God wanted was a creation in which there would be intelligent beings who, of their own volition, would love and serve Him. To have this, He had to create beings capable of making choices and give them the privilege of using that power. But to give such powers to created beings without limitations would soon take the universe out of God's control. So God has established a law of consequences whereby intelligent beings have the power and privilege of making choices, but with consequences attached to these choices over which they have no control.

**How does this account for the sorrow and suffering that is in the   69
world?**

All the sorrow and suffering in the world are part (though not
all) of the consequences of sin. God warned the man He created
that disobedience to His command would bring death. This involved, as later scriptures show, two forms of death. One is
spiritual death—separation from God; and that was immediate
and absolute. The moment Adam sinned he became spiritually
lost and spiritually dead. But physical death was also included.
Had God applied that part of the penalty at once, the human race
would have ended where it began; and it is altogether unlikely
that God would have created man in the first place, had He intended to destroy him so early in his experience. Instead God put
upon man the sentence of physical death but allowed him to live
over a long period of time before bringing that sentence to its
conclusion. In Adam's case, he lived 930 years (Gen 5:5).

This means that over a considerable period of time a person
lives under the sentence of death, with a law of death working in
his members, before he actually dies. We are told in the Bible
that God has set the number of man's days, and some live longer
than others. Some, of course, die in infancy, and we believe a
special provision is made for them. But in the meantime men are
subject to this law of death, and this includes sickness and various
forms of suffering. To eliminate this, God would have to bring
the sentence of death to its consummation. Many scriptures tell
us that God withholds the immediate execution of the sentence of
death to give men an opportunity to be saved. We are to "account that the longsuffering of our Lord is salvation," writes the
apostle Peter (2 Pe 3:15), and he adds that his fellow apostle,
Paul, had written the same thing.

**What about those who are saved, who have truly trusted in Christ   70
and are His followers? Do they not suffer with the rest?**

Yes, for if God were to bring judgment to consummation with
one, He would do so with all. A time is coming when God will
deal with living persons on earth to bring them into submission to
Himself. This time is usually referred to as the tribulation. This

does not refer to the fact of the trials of life which have always been common to man since the advent of sin, but the Lord Jesus described it as "great tribulation, such as was not since the beginning of the world to this time, no, nor ever shall be" (Mt 24:21). God will forgive the sins of those who turn to Him then, as He does now, but those who refuse to submit to Him in the face of these judgments will be destroyed. We do not mean annihilation but death, to be followed, eventually, by the final judgment of the great white throne of God, described in Revelation 20.

Until the appointed time of this tribulation (Ac 17:30-31), God bears with man's rebellion against Himself, and meantime man must bear with its consequences. When Christ brings all into subjection to Himself, He will establish His kingdom on earth which we commonly call the millennium, because we are told in Revelation 20 that it shall endure for a thousand years. Many scriptures, especially in the Old Testament, describe the conditions of universal peace and prosperity which shall prevail during that period.

71 **Is there any difference in God's dealings with the saved and unsaved?**

There is a sense in which God deals with all alike. The Lord Jesus said that God "maketh his sun to rise on the evil and on the good, and sendeth rain on the just and on the unjust" (Mt 5:45). If God causes a nation to prosper, saved and unsaved share in it alike, and participation is no proof of God's approval of the individual. Likewise in an epidemic Christians and non-Christians suffer alike, and being afflicted is no indication of God's disapproval.

Yet there is a difference, even though outward circumstances may be similar. In the case of the unsaved person, the one who does not commit his life to Christ in faith, acknowledging Him as Lord and Saviour, all the suffering is dead loss. It is endured without resulting gain. But those who are saved have the promise: "All things work together for good to them that love God, to them who are the called according to his purpose" (Ro 8:28). The immediate effect of suffering on the believer involves the disciplines of God, of which we read in Hebrews 12. We learn greater depths of the grace of God, and our lives are brought into conformity to Christ. Many believers have entered into profound communion with God while suffering pain or other adversity.

In God's long-range dealings with us, adverse circumstances are often overruled to our advantage, as in the life of Joseph and other Bible characters. There are many similar present-day experiences, so while not everything that happens is designed or approved by God, it is permitted by Him. He sets limits beyond which man may not go, and He also providentially overrules what happens to His children so that it works for our eventual blessing. Meantime these experiences bring us into conformity to the image of His Son who, in His life on earth, entered into all the sorrows common to man.

Can Man Thwart the Will of God?

If man has a free will and the privilege of choosing his course of action, is it not possible that he may frustrate the purposes of God? 72

God can and does overrule the actions of men to cause them to perform His purposes, but He does this, not by forcing them to do His will, but rather on the principle stated in the book of Job (5:13) and quoted by the apostle Paul, "He taketh the wise in their own craftiness" (1 Co 3:19). God does not prevent men from consummating their crafty designs, but He uses their actions to accomplish His purposes. This course of action glorifies God more, and more fully exposes the folly of sinful men.

It is in this connection that the apostle Paul writes, "The foolishness of God is wiser than men; and the weakness of God is stronger than men" (1 Co 1:25). It is not that God is either foolish or weak, but things appear so to fallen man's corrupted vision. Paul wrote of Christ: "Though he was crucified through weakness, yet he liveth by the power of God" (2 Co 13:4). Christ's death had all the appearance of weakness in the face of the opposition of men and Satan, yet God made His death the occasion of the atonement by laying on Him the iniquity of us all (Is

53:6). Hence when Christ rose from the dead, it was as Saviour of all who trust in Him and Judge of all who disbelieve and are opposed to Him.

73 Does the overruling of God to fulfill His will in any way mitigate the guilt or responsibility of His enemies, since what they do accomplishes His purposes?

No, and this is an interesting feature of this truth. Men are free to do their will, having their own motives; and they are accountable for both acts and motives. What God does through their acts is in spite of them and is in no way credited to them. We have a notable example of this in Acts 4:27-28: "For of a truth against thy holy child [or servant] Jesus, whom thou hast anointed, both Herod, and Pontius Pilate, with the Gentiles, and the people of Israel, were gathered together, for to do whatsoever thy hand and thy counsel determined before to be done." Since it was in the will of God to allow His Son to die a sacrificial death for our redemption, these persons and groups were actually serving His will. Yet it is plain that on their part it was not as servants of God, but, as verse 26 states, they "were gathered together against the Lord, and against his Christ."

Herod was a weak-willed man, a slave to his own passions and under the mastery of his wicked and strong-willed wife. He would not of himself have initiated the beheading of John the Baptist nor did he personally desire the death of Jesus. Yet he became the cause of the one and a party to the other by failing to exercise his legal prerogative to set the Lord Jesus free when he found no fault in Him. God did not predetermine that Herod should be the kind of man he was, but knowing him to be what he was, God used Herod's actions in fulfilling His will. Pilate likewise had no desire to put Jesus to death, and even washed his hands to symbolize his innocence; yet, in Acts 4 he receives special mention among those gathered together against Christ. We do not achieve innocence by washing our hands with water; cleansing from sin comes through the atoning blood of Christ (Rev 1:5-6).

Christ's enemies were expressing opposition to God, while He was expressing His infinite love for them in making His Son the sacrifice for sin. Both God's love and man's hatred were expressed in the same circumstances, but in the finality of things God's will was accomplished. The success of the powers of evil was temporary; the success of the purposes of God was eternal.

Could you give another example of this?   74

Yes, and in the same set of circumstances. In Matthew 20:18-19, while the Lord and His disciples were on their way to Jerusalem, He foretold what would happen there: "Behold, we go up to Jerusalem; and the Son of man shall be betrayed unto the chief priests and unto the scribes, and they shall condemn him to death, and shall deliver him to the Gentiles to mock, and to scourge, and to crucify him: and the third day he shall rise again." In this remarkable passage the Lord showed perfect insight into every detail of what awaited Him. Yet it all followed a natural pattern so that even those involved did not realize they were fulfilling the will of God. He would be arrested as the result of a betrayal, not to the Romans but to the Jews. He knew that they would condemn Him to death but instead of carrying out this sentence themselves, the Jews would deliver Him to the Romans to be crucified. The Jews' condemnation of Christ was because of what they considered His blasphemous claims to be the unique Son of God, but to the Romans they argued that He had made Himself a king and so opposed Caesar. Had our Lord's claim to be the Son of God been untrue, it would indeed have been blasphemy; but His resurrection vindicated that claim, as the apostle Paul states in Romans 1:4: He was "declared to be the Son of God with power, according to the spirit of holiness, by the resurrection from the dead."

Why were these circumstances important?   75

Had the Jews killed Jesus they would have stoned Him, but they did not do so, for they did not want to become ceremonially defiled by such an involvement, which would have prevented their participation in the celebration of the Passover. Hence they insisted that the Romans perform the execution, even though Pilate did not wish to do so. If the Jews had stoned Jesus, they would have invalidated a number of prophecies concerning His death. The stoning would in all probability have broken some bones, but Scripture had said, "A bone of him shall not be broken" (Jn 19:36; see Ps 34:20). And they would not have pierced Him, but Scripture said this would be done (Jn 19:37; see Zec 12:10). Psalm 22 describes the death of Christ as exposing Him physically to those passing by while He suffered agony and thirst. None of this would have been accomplished had the Jews stoned Him.

Their professed reason for not carrying out the execution themselves was that Roman law forbade their executing anyone. Yet in the case of Stephen they had no inhibition. We read that in the midst of his trial, "they cried out with a loud voice, and stopped their ears, and ran upon him with one accord, and cast him out of the city, and stoned him" (Ac 7:57-58). But also involved in these circumstances is the fact that God so ordered things that both Jews and Gentiles participated in putting His Son to death, and even the two rulers were representatives of these two groups. Pilate represented the intruding power of Rome, while the Herodian family, though not Jewish, was tied in with the people of Israel by the marriage of Herod the Great to a granddaughter of a former high priest.

How Can I Know the Will of God for My Life?

76   How does one go about finding the will of God for his life?

God reveals Himself to men in various ways, and these have a bearing on His will for our lives. He reveals Himself in creation, and natural laws must be observed and obeyed. He reveals Himself in the Bible, and its instructions must be followed. He reveals Himself in His Son, and His example and precepts are a pattern for those who trust Him as their Saviour. God also reveals Himself in the lives of His children, and sometimes one finds God's will, partly at least, in counseling with fellow-believers. Sometimes we find His will through His providential dealings with us.

Where should one start in determining the will of God for his life?

He must begin with the personal acknowledgment of Jesus Christ as Lord of his life. It is God's will that all men should be saved and come to the knowledge of the truth (1 Ti 2:3-4), and if we have not taken this step of submitting our lives to Him, we are out of the will of God completely. There is no possibility of finding God's will so long as we fail to take the initial step of acknowledging Jesus Christ as Lord and Saviour. The Bible says we are born with sinful natures (Eph 2:3) and that we must be born again in order to become children of God in the biblical sense of the term (Jn 1:12; 3:3). Once we have taken this step we are in a position to seek and find the rest of His will for us. Ephesians 2:10 tells us that in the new birth we are "created in Christ Jesus unto good works, which God has before ordained that we should walk in them." This shows that God has a plan and purpose for the life of every believer.

Is there any particular sequence in the things mentioned which we should follow to learn God's will?

No sequence is absolute, and sometimes God leads one of His children differently from the way He leads another. We can never limit the working of God to our form of logic: "For my thoughts are not your thoughts, neither are your ways my ways, saith the Lord. For as the heavens are higher than the earth, so are my ways higher than your ways, and my thoughts than your thoughts" (Is 55:8-9). It is not for us to determine how God must act but rather to follow as He leads.

Yet in a general way I think it is safe to say that if we have taken the first, absolutely essential step of receiving Christ as our Saviour, we should seek His will further in the Bible, God's authoritative revelation of Himself. The Lord Jesus said, "Heaven and earth shall pass away, but my words shall not pass away" (Mt 24:35). It is here that we find the history of God's dealings with men, the way of salvation, prophecies of things to come, as well as instructions for living. These constitute "a lamp shining in a dark place," as Peter puts it (2 Pe 1:19, alt. trans.), and are always relevant. While the mode of living varies in different parts of the earth and from one century to another, biblical instruction retains its relevancy because it relates to man's basic spiritual needs rather than defining a particular code of mores to govern all peoples of all times.

79   Does the Bible give guidance for every detail of life?

Not always explicitly, though it covers a wide range of instruction, either by precept or example. Sometimes guidance is given in the form of a principle, often illustrated by example. An instance of instruction by principle is: "Whether therefore ye eat, or drink, or whatsoever ye do, do all to the glory of God" (1 Co 10:31). This shows that a fundamental consideration of the propriety of an act is to determine whether it will be in keeping with our witness as a Christian or whether it may rather be a discredit to Christ, whose name we bear. This will often lead to a decision which is not precisely defined in the Bible but which is in conformity to God's will. An example is found in the life of Daniel, who refused to eat food which, in the custom of the times, would have been in some way involved in idol worship.

Our perfect example is seen in the life of Christ. At the beginning of His public ministry He submitted to the testing of Satan, who first suggested that in view of Christ's long fast, He prove His deity by performing a miracle, commanding that the stones become bread for Him to eat. Christ's answer was a quotation from Deuteronomy 8:3: "Man shall not live by bread alone, but by every word that proceedeth out of the mouth of God" (Mt 4:4). One who lives by the Word of God does not act on challenges by others but moves by the leading of the Holy Spirit, in conformity with God's Word.

But many things are clearly and simply defined in the Bible, such as the instruction not to be unequally yoked together with unbelievers (2 Co 6:14). Another is the commandment: "that ye should abstain from fornication" (1 Th 4:3), as well as the Ten Commandments (Ex 20:1-17), including, "Thou shalt not commit adultery." The entire list of commandments needs a re-emphasis in these days when many advocate what is called "the new morality," based on expediency and ignoring the fact that it is God with whom we have to do. Romans 14:12 says, "Every one of us shall give account of himself to God," and it will be on the basis of His standards. The New Testament amplifies the bearing of these commandments, showing that they apply to our thoughts as well as to our acts and words. There can be no question of what is God's will in matters like these.

You mentioned God's providences. Could you give an example   80
of these?

Yes, we have a notable one in the case of Gideon, one of the judges in the early days of Israel's history. He asked of God a sign (Judg 6:36-40), and the Lord granted him a specific sign. But this kind of guidance is precarious, since we cannot always be sure the events were not a coincidence. Gideon himself experienced this difficulty, as the passage shows, and he requested the sign in reverse before he felt assured it was truly God's answer. In the New Testament we find the apostle Paul and his party being guided, in part at least, by certain providences of God (Ac 16:6-10). The expression "assuredly gathering" (v. 10) suggests also that the members of the group consulted together, arriving at a conclusion. God may guide in various ways but never in contravention of His written Word, the Bible.

Are Christian Parents Responsible if Their Children Do Not Turn Out Well?

In the so-called "generation gap" parents are often counted re-   81
sponsible for the attitudes of their children: is this a valid claim?

To some degree, obviously, parents have a responsibility for their children. But there are limits to this, since each person is a distinct individual with his or her own mind and separate accountability to God. We are responsible for the way we have dealt with our children in rearing them, but we cannot always be held responsible for what our offspring may do in later life. It is not easy to differentiate and evaluate the comparative degrees of responsibility of parents and children, but we believe it is wrong to assume that parents can control the mind and personality of their children. In fact, we do not believe life was meant to be that way, otherwise children would simply be replicas of their parents. A basic truth of the Bible is individual accountability to God as we read in Romans 14:12, "So then every one of us shall give account of himself to God." In the finality of things no one can be held responsible for another.

82   Can Christian parents assure the salvation of their offspring?

Many hold this statement to be true, but there are some serious obstacles to this belief. They use Acts 16:31 as a proof text, and complain when the last clause is omitted, as is frequently the case: "Believe on the Lord Jesus Christ, and thou shalt be saved, and thy house." It is more correctly, "*Thou* and thy house." To take this verse as a promise (that if he would believe, not only he but all his house, *i.e.*, his family, would be saved) would make their salvation contingent on *his* faith as head of the house. New birth, however, is never by families but by individual faith in Christ. Nor is the teaching any more acceptable to add (though Scripture does not) that he must live a godly life and teach his family the Word of God. In no case in the Bible does the faith of one avail for another or assure that that person will share his faith. Often several children in a family become saved, while others do not, whether the parents are saved or not. There is no universal rule. We take this text to signify that not only could the jailer be saved but also his family. His thoughts had quite naturally centered in his own need, whereas Paul and Silas saw the opportunity of reaching the larger circle of his family. The balance of the chapter indicates that the entire household turned to Christ in faith.

83   Are there not promises made to Christian parents, or heads of houses, with regard to God blessing their home and family?

Yes, there are many precious promises along this line, though not including the salvation of the household. Another text often

used to support the idea that parents can assure the salvation of
their children is Proverbs 22:6: "Train up a child in the way he
should go: and when he is old, he will not depart from it." When
children turn out badly parents have not necessarily failed to
bring them up properly. No set pattern exists for bringing up children; in the same family some turn to the Lord and others do not.
Parents can help by godly lives and spiritual counsel, to the best
of their understanding of the circumstances and relationships involved. But sometimes even where parents are very remiss, children will give themselves to the Lord. In other cases in spite of
much prayer and love in the home, they do not do so. Yet it *is* a
general principle that godly training in early life leaves its mark
on the child and often results in conversion to Christ. This, we
believe, is all the verse is meant to teach. It is a statement of
principle, rather than a specific promise.

Does this mean that parents are not at all responsible for their 84
children?

By no means, except that *ultimate* responsibility lies within
each person. But there runs through Scripture a teaching that
each of us has responsibility, not only for misdeeds, but also for
our failure to act when we should. On the positive side, "every
transgression and disobedience receives a just recompence of
reward" (Heb 2:2); while on the negative side: "To him that
knoweth to do good, and doeth it not, to him it is sin"(Ja 4:17).
If we have neglected the spiritual instruction of our children,
we are accountable to God for this omission. Included is failure
to set a good example before them since children learn more from
example than from precept. We must also be concerned about
their spiritual welfare, seeking to win them to Christ. A similar
principle is stated in Ezekiel 3:17-21 (and repeated in 33:7-9),
that while those who die in their sins are responsible for their attitude and relationship to God, yet if we have not done our part to
warn them of impending judgment, we also will be held responsible for our failure in this respect.

85 **How does this apply to those who profess Christianity in a general way, but have not made a definite commitment of themselves to Christ by personal faith in Him?**

Such a condition is a very serious one and has much to do with the delinquency of our day. To profess Christianity as a religion without a personal commitment of ourselves to Christ in faith gives ground for an oft-heard accusation that all Christians are hypocrites. The accusation is false, but many people do not realize that there is a distinction between those who are Christian by conviction, and those to whom it is at best a mild preference over other religions. People of other countries are often perplexed because they consider the United States of America to be a Christian country. Having learned from missionaries or other committed Christians something of what Christianity involves, they are amazed to find a complete contradiction by what they see and hear when they visit our land.

The same applies to children who are brought up in the United States. They hear a great deal about Christian truth and Christian love, and often find it completely contradicted by what they see and hear. Those who make an empty profession of faith in Christ do bear a heavy responsibility both as regards their own state of unbelief, and also for the effect their position and attitude have on others. But we must recognize that when we give account of ourselves to God we cannot blame things on the hypocrisy of another. The birth and life and death of Christ are evidence of God's love for us, and Christ's resurrection assures the salvation of those who trust in Him (Ro 4:25).

What Is the Relation of Faith and Works in Christianity?

86 **One hears much controversy about faith and works; how are they related in the Bible?**

A simple rule is that works which are acceptable to God follow faith, and those which precede faith do not have merit in His sight. No work of ours before or after our coming to Christ in faith has any merit with regard to *salvation.* We are saved solely by Christ's atonement; hence, "by grace through faith" (Eph 2:8-9). "By grace" means that it is free of any charge or requirement of merit. "Through faith" means that we accept Christ by a volitional act, so that we are in that act acknowledging both our spiritual bankruptcy and the efficacy of Christ's atoning blood. The Bible does not speak of our making a meritorious contribution to our salvation. To introduce this idea would be false doctrine. In 1 Corinthians 15:1-4 the apostle Paul declared the gospel *which he preached, which they believed,* and *by which they were saved.* This declaration speaks only of Christ's death and resurrection on our behalf and says nothing of any work on our part. To make the matter more emphatic, Paul wrote in Galatians 1:8-9 that if even an angel from heaven preached any other gospel than that which he had preached and they had believed, "let him be accursed."

Is there any way to simplify the subject? 87

We believe so. The New Testament speaks of four categories of works: wicked works, dead works, good works, and works of faith. Colossians 1:21 says that we were alienated from God and enemies to Him in our mind by wicked works. Galatians 5:19-21 describes some of the things which constitute wicked works: adultery, fornication, uncleanness, envyings, murders, drunkenness, and so on, which are well-known and easily recognized.

"Dead works" are not so readily recognized, since we take the term to refer to works which in themselves are not wicked, but actually good. Yet since they are done before conversion to Christ they have no merit with regard to salvation. The building of hospitals and libraries, often done by philanthropists who have not personally submitted themselves to God in repentance for sin and through faith in Christ, may be taken as an example of such works. Acts of kindness on which many rely for their hope of being saved are also included. But none of these things can put away sin. The Lord Jesus said, "Except a man be born again, he cannot see the kingdom of God" (Jn 3:3). Hebrews 6:1 and

9:14 teach that dead works are to be repented of in order that we may "serve the living God." Nicodemus was a ruler of the Jews, and is believed to have been a man of good character and high integrity, yet he was told by the Lord that he needed to be born again. Likewise the rich young ruler claimed to have kept the law of Moses from his youth, but he himself realized that there was something lacking. The Lord's answer showed him that on the ground he took he was not saved. We cannot expiate our sins by any amount of good works.

88   Both of these categories, wicked works and dead works, are unacceptable to God. How would you describe the others which are acceptable to God?

"Good works" are works of rectitude or of beneficence. In Matthew 26:10 the Lord says of the woman who anointed Him at the feast shortly before His crucifixion (whom we take to be Mary of Bethany), "she hath wrought a good work upon me." The anointing at the end of the meal did not constitute a benefit bestowed upon Him but was an expression of her love for Him and was symbolic of a spirit of worship. It was fitting and right that she should perform this act; it had great value in His sight, not with regard to salvation, but as an act of devotion on the part of one already saved. This category may well include what we might term religious acts, such as church attendance, reading the Bible, prayer, and so on.

There are also works of beneficence, such as ministering to the physical needs of others. Serving the Lord is not always to be identified with preaching. We witness to the love of God by acts of kindness and mercy, and quite often people are won to the Lord in this way who would not listen to preaching. The scene in Matthew 25:31-46 shows how the Lord accepts that kind of witness as evidence of an underlying faith on the part of those He addresses, though it should be noted that their acts were done during the tribulation period, when it may well have been at the risk of their lives to have so acted.

What about the last category, works of faith; how would you describe them? 89

These are acts which have not to do with either rectitude or beneficence. For example, when Peter challenged the Lord to bid him come on the water and the Lord did so, Peter's getting out of the boat into the sea was neither moral nor immoral, nor did it do anyone any good. Yet no act could have given stronger demonstration of his faith in the Lord Jesus and in the power of His word. An act of faith is not predicated on the good it will do, though it may have that character, but is primarily acting on the Word of God in the confidence that it will serve God's will. When Moses by faith refused to be called the son of Pharaoh's daughter no one was immediately benefited, least of all himself. Yet it was the strongest demonstration of the reality of his belief in God, and in the promises made to the fathers of Israel, even though there was no written word to go by until Moses himself began the writing of the sacred volume years later.

But does not the Bible speak of being justified by works? 90

It does, indeed, and the latter half of James 2 is devoted to expounding this subject. He speaks of one who says he has faith but whose life does not correspond to his profession. He says the claim is empty unless substantiated by works. His first illustration involves the element of "good works," as well as substantiating faith. If a person says to one who is cold and destitute, "Be ye warmed and fed," but gives him no help, it is like a profession of faith in words only with no evidence of reality. The balance of the chapter is devoted to showing that the only way we can demonstrate faith, and so be justified before men in the claim we make, is to act on the convictions we profess.

Abraham was willing to offer up his only son, through whom God said He would give Abraham a posterity, before that son was ever married, in the conviction that God would raise him from the dead (Heb 11:17-19). This, James avers, justified Abraham by works. But long before that incident (related in Gen 22) God had declared Abraham to be justified by faith (Gen 15:6). Works are neither a substitute nor a supplement for faith.

They accomplish a different purpose. Justification before God is on the ground of our faith (Ro 4:1-5) while justification before men is on the ground of our works. The justifying works are the outward evidence of the reality of inborn faith which is the ground on which *God* justifies. "For by grace are ye saved through faith; and that not of yourselves: it is the gift of God: not of works, lest any man should boast" (Eph 2:8-9).

What Is Christian Liberty?

91   In what way does the Bible proclaim liberty to humanity?

Basically the message of the Bible is freedom from sin. This is the meaning of the often quoted but frequently misapplied words of the Lord Jesus Christ: "Ye shall know the truth, and the truth shall make you free" (Jn 8:32). He was not speaking of academic knowledge or of truth in an abstract and philosophical way. He had just said to those who professed to believe on Him, "If ye continue in my word, then are ye my disciples indeed" (Jn 8:31). The "truth" to which He referred was the revealed truth of God, contained in the Bible. In the discussion which followed His statement, those present thought He referred to political freedom, but He said plainly: "Whosoever committeth sin is the servant [or slave] of sin" (8:34). Unless men are delivered from the bondage of sin they cannot fully enjoy other kinds of liberty. What many people think of as liberty is simply the permissiveness which allows them to indulge in any kind of sin without restraint or retribution. This is not true liberty, but rather anarchy; and it leads to chaos. Freedom from sin permits an ordered and cooperative society. It enables us to live for the glory of God and for the common good of man.

92   Does the Bible teach liberty on the human level between men and nations?

Yes. Though in many respects God permits men to pursue their own aims and purposes which do not make for peace, yet He has never relinquished His overruling providence, so that in the end, men reap what they sow. God's purposes will be carried out, and this will eventuate in peace on earth and good will among men. Satan claimed to have power to appoint the rulers of the kingdoms of the earth, Luke 4:6, yet Daniel 4:17 says that God purposes "that the living may know that the Most High ruleth in the kingdom of men, and giveth it to whomsoever he will, and setteth up over it the basest of men." Consequently God holds rulers to certain standards. God said to David: "He that ruleth over men must be just, ruling in the fear of God" (2 Sa 23:3).

David admitted that he did not himself live up to this and the Bible shows that he suffered judgments from God on this account. The Bible teaches the equality of men before God. While it directs the establishment of governmental authority and instructs us to be subject to "the powers that be," yet it nowhere sanctions the capricious use of arbitrary force. Where this is done it is in violation of all the instructions in the Bible which inculcate mutual respect and justice to be measured to all persons alike. History shows that where the Bible has been respected and obeyed, men live in peace.

What is the origin of the text molded on what we call the "liberty 93
bell"?

The text is part of Leviticus 25:10: "Proclaim liberty throughout all the land unto all the inhabitants thereof." Its use on the bell was a religious-political sentiment which reflected the spiritual outlook of the times. It was not cast for use in proclaiming American independence of England, but was ordered in 1751 for use in the celebration by the Pennsylvania provincial council of the golden jubilee of William Penn's Charter of Privileges, issued in 1701. The bell arrived in Philadelphia in 1752. It became cracked while being tested for tone and had to be recast twice. It was rung on July 8, 1776, in connection with the proclamation of the Declaration of Independence which had been signed four days earlier. The bell and its text are commonly considered a symbol of the political freedom enjoyed in the United States of America.

94   Was the placing of the text on the bell politically motivated?

No. It was probably inspired by the event it was first intended to celebrate. But that was a *fait accompli*, and not a cause to be supported. There was at that time no thought of secession from Great Britain. The name Liberty Bell was first used by an anti-slavery group in 1839, almost a century after the bell was originally ordered. Yet there seemed a providential guidance in having this particular text made part of the bell which not only celebrated the liberties already enjoyed, but which later had such a prominent place in the proclamation that "We hold these Truths to be self-evident, that all Men are created equal, that they are endowed by their Creator with certain inalienable Rights, that among these are Life, Liberty, and the Pursuit of Happiness—That to secure these Rights, Governments are instituted among Men, deriving their just Powers from the Consent of the Governed."

We believe it noteworthy that the signers of the declaration believed that government was instituted to secure the rights of the inhabitants of the land, not to oppress them. However, we might dispute the statement that government derives its just powers from the consent of the governed. The apostle Paul declares that "The powers that be are ordained of God" (Ro 13:1). All authority, all right of government, rests with God, and men have authority only insofar as it is delegated to them by God. Those in authority do well to remember this.

95   How can we, and should we, proclaim liberty today?

Spiritual liberty, which is the root of all true liberty, is proclaimed in the gospel message. Peter declared long ago, in the home of the Roman soldier Cornelius, "To him [Christ] give all the prophets witness, that through his name whosoever believeth in him shall receive remission of sins" (Ac 10:43). And the Lord Jesus declared, "If the Son therefore shall make you free, ye shall be free indeed" (Jn 8:36). This makes possible life at its highest level, no matter what conditions may prevail around us.

Christians in various countries live under conditions that are less than ideal, and it has always been so. Neither the Lord Jesus nor the apostles organized movements against the existing order, though in their personal lives they stood for right, and against evil. Since Christianity is not confined to any particular country, or political party, or social stratum, mixing the cause of Christ with political movements could lead to confusion which would mar the effectiveness of Christian testimony. If we earnestly seek man's spiritual good, we cannot be unmindful of his physical and material needs. Scripture leads us to be concerned for others, while recognizing the overriding importance of the things which are eternal.

What Is Christian Fellowship?

Many things are described as having "fellowship." What does 96 this word mean in the Christian's vocabulary?

The word usually translated "fellowship" is *koinōnia*, which means, simply, to have things in common. It quite naturally finds application to a variety of circumstances and conditions. Because of this many become confused about its essential meaning. The basic Christian fellowship is between the believer and each of the Persons of the Holy Trinity; second to that is fellowship with Christians. The apostle John wrote: "That which we have seen and heard declare we unto you, that ye also might have fellowship with us: and truly our fellowship is with the Father, and with his Son Jesus Christ" (1 Jn 1:3). Paul adds, in 2 Corinthians 13:14: "The grace of the Lord Jesus Christ, and the love of God, and the communion of the Holy Ghost, be with you all. Amen." The word translated "communion" is the one translated "fellowship" elsewhere. John made known to his readers the things concerning the Father and the Son that we might share them, and be brought into the experience of a life lived in communion with God as our Father, and the Lord Jesus Christ, His Son, as our Saviour. Paul taught much about the Holy Spirit indwelling believers, and speaks of our communion with Him. John also speaks of our having fellowship with one another, as those who walk in the light of God.

97   What does this fellowship involve?

It means that we share in the knowledge of God, and of His purposes and feelings. In the new birth God communicates His life to us, and as that life matures, we learn about His nature. Through the study of His Word we share His thinking which includes not only His planning, but also the understanding of what pleases and what displeases Him. This goes beyond the mere knowledge of these things, and leads us to experience the same feelings—to love what He loves, and hate what He hates. It is this fellowship with God which makes possible the fellowship of saints, for it is only as the divine thoughts and feelings supersede those which are natural with us that people of totally diverse backgrounds can live and work together in the close family relationship which exists among the children of God. As we live in communion with God the life of Christ is reproduced in us.

98   In what does fellowship among saints consist?

This takes many forms, from the purely spiritual to what is largely mundane. One is sharing in the worship and service of the church. The remembrance of the Lord in the breaking of bread has been the symbol of church fellowship from the very beginning. "The cup of blessing which we bless, is it not the communion of the blood of Christ? The bread which we break, is it not the communion of the body of Christ" (1 Co 10:16). In this sense "fellowship" is in the nature of membership. Some groups which disclaim the idea of membership nevertheless speak freely of those who are "in fellowship." Acts 9:26-28 gives warrant for such recognition, whatever we may call it.

Usually those who participate in the Lord's Supper, or Holy Communion, are considered to be in the recognized fellowship of the group, or at least such recognition is open to them. But were we to limit the thought of fellowship to participation in an external rite it would not express the full sense of the word. Paul expressed appreciation for the fellowship of the Philippians in the work of the gospel "from the first day until now" (Phil 1:5). He amplified this by saying they had helped to support him (Phil 4:15-17). Fellowship in the work of the Lord includes supporting it by prayer and financial contribution, as well as attending services where possible, and having any part in communicating the good news of salvation through faith in Christ to those who are still in their sins. In Galatians 2:9 the apostles at Jerusalem showed their fellowship with Paul and Barnabas by expressing confidence in the fact that God had called them to work among the Gentiles.

Can fellowship be expressed in material ways? 99

Very definitely. We often hear of a fellowship supper being held. As we share God's provision in the meal, we also share in giving thanks to Him; and it is an occasion when we rejoice together, and often share our experiences in the Christian life. Throughout man's history, and throughout the Bible, sharing a meal has been the occasion of fostering friendship. In the case of Christians it fosters mutual love, and a better understanding of one another. It would be very shallow holiness which would consider this too mundane to be considered an expression of Christian fellowship. It is sometimes followed by a hymn sing. Something of this kind seems to be indicated in Acts 2:46, where they broke bread from house to house, and did eat their food with gladness and singleness of heart. The formal "breaking of bread" seems to be referred to in verse 42, but verse 46 was the sharing in a common meal. It was something in the nature of the "love feast," which Paul describes in 1 Corinthians 11, although there it immediately preceded the formal observance of the Lord's Supper. The word fellowship has a broad scope, and can include anything we have in common. The same word in a different form was used for the *partnership* between Simon Peter and the brothers, James and John.

What are some of the other uses of the word "fellowship" in the Bible? 100

In Romans 15:26 the contribution made to the poor saints of Judea is described by this term in the Greek text. It constituted a sharing of material possessions, and was an expression of the love of Christ on the part of these believers. The word can be used in a wide variety of circumstances. An unusual one is where

Paul expressed the desire to know the fellowship of Christ's sufferings: "That I may know him, and the power of his resurrection, and the fellowship of his sufferings, being made conformable unto his death" (Phil 3:10). The sharing of the sufferings of Christ makes possible greater sharing in His glory (Ro 8:17). This does not refer to Christ's atoning sufferings, which He bore alone (Heb 1:3), but to the sufferings which He left behind for us (Col 1:24).

Fellowship with one another is evidence of fellowship with God (1 Jn 4:20; 5:1). We can have the first without the second, but we cannot be in fellowship with God while remaining at odds with our fellow believers. An unforgiving spirit toward others hinders God's forgiveness to us (Mt 6:14-15, etc.). Our fruitfulness to God depends on our being in close fellowship with Him (Jn 15:4-5). We are saved as individuals (Ro 14:12), but united to fellow believers as members of the body of Christ (1 Co 12:13; Col 3:15).

THE PERSON OF CHRIST

Does the Bible Teach That Jesus Christ Is God?

Some religions take credit for the fact that they do not deify their **101**
founder. Are we wrong in claiming that Jesus Christ is God?

It is not only wrong but impossible to deify a person, although, of course, it can be *claimed* that a person is God when he is not. This has been done many times throughout human history. This accusation was leveled at Jesus many times while He lived. For example, after the Jews had challenged Him: "If thou be the Christ, tell us plainly" (Jn 10:24), He replied, "I told you, and ye believed not: the works that I do in my Father's name, they bear witness of me. I and my Father are one" (vv. 25, 30). We are then told that "the Jews took up stones again to stone him. Jesus answered them, Many good works have I showed you from my Father; for which of those works do ye stone me? The Jews answered him, saying, For a good work we stone thee not; but for blasphemy; and because that thou, being a man, makest thyself God" (vv. 31-33).

Had this last statement been true, it would, indeed, have been blasphemy, but the fact was just the reverse. Scripture teaches that He subsisted as God before His incarnation and that He *became man.* Christ is presented in the Bible as being eternally existent. While Christianity holds to monotheism, as does Judaism, it teaches that God subsists in three Persons—Father, Son, and Holy Spirit, all sharing the same life and nature, each having the same attributes, and all working harmoniously so that to each is attributed part in creation and redemption. It is on this ground that the Lord Jesus said, "I and my Father are one."

102 How does the Bible teach that God is a Trinity?

Not by direct statement, for the word "trinity" is not found in the Bible. But divine attributes are ascribed to each of the Persons of the Holy Trinity. To each is ascribed eternity of being, creative power, omnipotence, omniscience, omnipresence, and the same character of love and holiness. The Persons of the Deity are given equality in references to Them which would be entirely incongruous were any of Them less than God. Any two or all three of Them are referred to together but are never associated with any inferior being. These things justify our acceptance of the fact that the Bible presents God as a Holy Trinity.

103 Is Jesus ever addressed as God in the Bible or is He ever so described in any passage?

Numerous passages identify Jesus as God, sometimes directly and sometimes indirectly. He is often called Son of God. This does not imply generation but rather that He stands in relationship to the Father as a unique Son.

However Jesus is addressed directly as God in Hebrews 1:8, where a quotation from Psalm 45:6 is identified as having Him in view: "But unto the Son he saith, Thy throne, O God, is forever and ever: a scepter of righteousness is the scepter of thy kingdom." In 1 John 5:20 it is said of Him: "This is the true God, and eternal life." He is declared to *be* God in the opening verses of John's Gospel: "In the beginning was the Word, and the Word was with God, and the Word was God. The same was in the beginning with God. All things were made by him; and without him was not anything made that was made" (1:1-3).

In many other passages also Jesus is identified as God. Philippians 2:6 tells us that before His incarnation He was "in the form of God"; and in Colossians 1:16-17 He is declared to be the Creator and Sustainer of all things. That epistle states that "in him dwelleth all the fullness of the Godhead bodily" (2:9). Numerous Old Testament passages which refer to Jehovah are identified in the New Testament as having application to Christ. One such passage is found in the opening verses of Isaiah 6, where Isaiah says he "saw also the Lord sitting upon a throne, high and lifted up, and his train filled the temple." In verse 3 the seraphim salute this Person by saying, "Holy, holy, holy, is the Lord [Jehovah] of hosts: the whole earth is full of his glory." The apostle John identifies this Person with Jesus: "These things said Esaias [Isaiah] when he saw his [Christ's] glory, and spake of him" (Jn 12:41).

If the New Testament teaches that God is a Holy Trinity, does 104 this not deny the monotheism of the Old Testament?

No, it does not. Monotheism simply insists that there is *one* living and true God, but it does not define the being of God. It stands in contrast, not with the trinitarian teaching of the New Testament, but with the polytheism of many other religions, especially in those days when various forms of idolatry and animism were widely held. In recent years the idea of monotheism has become more widely accepted, but especially in ancient times many believed in a multiplicity of gods, as some still do today. There were gods of the land and gods of the sea; gods of the wind and gods of the rain and of the various elements of nature; there were gods of the hills and gods of the valleys; gods of the sun, moon and various planets; gods of the living and gods of the dead. This wide variety of gods instilled fear into people in connection with almost every experience of life.

Not only does the Bible teach that all of this is vain and false and that there is only one living and true God, but it also reveals Him as a God of justice, purity, and love. He is neither capricious nor unjust. At the same time, it makes clear that it is He to whom "everyone of us shall give account of himself" (Ro 14:12). It teaches the fear of God in the sense of reverence rather than dread, unless we rebel against Him. Then we might well fear Him in the most dreadful sense.

If God is a Trinity, does this ever lead to a conflict of interest on 105 the part of the Persons of the Godhead?

No. Since each is equally endowed with the divine mind and nature there could never be any conflict of interest, though they may function differently. It is characteristic of the Persons of the Trinity to work in harmony and cooperation in all that they undertake, much as our body works in harmony with our mind and will if we are in normal health. Scripture suggests that the divine purposes are formed by mutual consent, as we read in Genesis 1:26: "God said, Let us make man in our image, after our likeness. . . ."

Is Christ the Hope of the World?

106 We often hear it said that Christ is the hope of the world. What biblical basis is there for this statement?

This claim is often made without explaining in what way, or by what means Christ is the hope of the world, and this results in frustration. The claim continues to be made; yet the world plunges on into deeper distress. Efforts to establish a peaceful economy of nations fail because of the aggressions of some; and when others oppose that aggression they are themselves often labeled aggressors. Efforts to right social wrongs fail of fulfillment, while in many cases, those supposedly being helped feel that the help is misdirected. At best injustices are shifted rather than being corrected. People wonder how Christ fits into the picture, and many doubt that Christianity has any solution for the problems of mankind today.

107 Didn't the angels speak of "peace on earth, good will toward men" in connection with Christ's birth?

Yes, but it should be noticed that the statement was made in connection with the presence on earth of the One who is called in prophecy the Prince of Peace. It was the occasion of the incarnation of the Son of God, toward whom all prophecy pointed. But when He came to maturity and entered upon His public ministry, instead of freeing the nation Israel from the yoke of Rome, as they expected their promised Messiah to do, He made it clear that God must first deal with the sins of mankind. This was an aspect the patriots of that time did not take into consideration. They wanted a leader who would bring them political liberty, but they were not concerned about getting their personal lives into line with God's will.

John the Baptist was the authorized forerunner of the Lord
Jesus, according to the angel's statement to John's father, Zacha-
rias the priest (Lk 1:17). John's message to the nation brought
up the unwelcome subject of sin: "Repent ye: for the kingdom of
heaven is at hand" (Mt 3:2). While many responded, the mass
of the nation did not, and least of all, their leaders. The outcome
was that Jesus was rejected and His crucifixion was demanded by
the leaders of the nation, though it was the Romans who actually
crucified Him. In the prayer recorded in Acts 4 we are told that
"Herod, and Pontius Pilate, with the Gentiles, and the people of
Israel" were gathered together against Christ. This puts the
responsibility for His crucifixion upon us all, and it helps to
explain why there cannot now be that "peace on earth, good will
toward men" for which men long.

Does this mean there will never be peace on earth?   108

No, because such a condition is definitely prophesied in several places in Scripture. The Bible tells in almost poetical language of a time when men "shall beat their swords into plowshares, and their spears into pruning-hooks: nation shall not lift
up sword against nation, neither shall they learn war any more"
(Is 2:4). It also speaks of this as a time when the blight of sin's
curse shall be removed from the earth, so that it no longer will
bring forth thorns and thistles, but rather, as we read in Psalm
67:6-7, "Then shall the earth yield her increase; and God, even
our own God, shall bless us. God shall bless us; and all the ends
of the earth shall fear him."

There will be a time of universal peace and prosperity, and
Scripture even indicates that in that age the span of human life
will be increased, perhaps even beyond what it was in the early
ages of human experience. According to the early chapters of
Genesis, many men at that time lived to an age beyond nine
hundred years, and Scripture says that in the millennial kingdom
of Christ there will be no deaths except under the judgment of
God for unrepented sin. This will be man's long dreamed of
"golden age"; but it lies in the future after a second advent of
Christ. Many are unaware that the Bible speaks more about the
second advent of Christ than it does of the first, and in referring

to it, Peter says, "We have also a more sure word of prophecy" (2 Pe 1:19). Some translate this, "the word of prophecy confirmed." We take this to mean that since the prophecies of Christ's first advent were fulfilled literally, we have added reason to expect that those concerning His second advent will also be fulfilled literally. Peter assures us that his message was not a cunningly devised fable, and that neither was he deluded in proclaiming it nor was he deluding us. But men cannot, by their own power, bring this about. It will require the exercise of divine power, putting down sin and iniquity.

109 What hope does Christianity hold out to men today?

Today God is offering men individual salvation—the forgiveness of sins through faith in Christ and the impartation of a new life in the regenerating power of the Holy Spirit. When men crucified His Son, God made it the occasion of bringing about the atonement. We read in Isaiah 53:6, "The LORD [Jehovah] hath laid on him the iniquity of us all." The apostle Paul explains this in his letter to the Romans (3:24-26): "Being justified freely by his grace through the redemption that is in Christ Jesus: whom God hath set forth to be a propitiation through faith in his blood, to declare his righteousness for the remission of sins that are past, through the forbearance of God; to declare . . . at this time his righteousness: that he might be just, and the justifier of him which believeth in Jesus."

No doubt where a large proportion of society avail themselves of this provision there will be an improvement in social life, and in the relations of nations to one another, within the sphere in which such influence is felt. But where Christ is rejected and men choose indulgence in sin, called by whatever euphemism, we must accept the dictum of God: "There is no peace, saith my God, to the wicked" (Is 57:21). In such circumstances Christ is not the hope of the world but rather stands as the judge of all the earth. But His saving grace is open to all mankind, giving us "everlasting consolation and good hope through grace," as we read in 2 Thessalonians 2:16.

Why Was Jesus Baptized?

If the baptism of John was for repentance, why was Jesus bap- 110 tized, since He was sinless?

One purpose of the baptism of John was to provide a divinely appointed mode whereby the people of his day might acknowledge repentance for sin, but this was not the only purpose. In the gospel of Luke we are given an account of the birth of John and the nature and purpose of his ministry. We are told first of all some background facts of his ancestry and circumstances leading to his birth. His parents were a godly couple, a Levitical priest and his wife, advanced in years. Their prayers for a child had not been answered. One day as the husband was completing his functions of priesthood, an angel appeared and revealed that their prayers would be answered; God would give them a son whom they were to name John ("grace of Jehovah"). Zachariah was told that the child would be the personal forerunner of the long-promised Messiah. Consequently John would be filled with the Holy Spirit from the day of his birth (Lk 1:15), and on their part they were to see that the child observed the Nazarite vow of separation to God as outlined in Numbers 6:2-6. After the child was weaned we read that he was in the deserts till he began his public ministry.

At the time appointed by God we read that the word of the Lord came to John (Lk 3:2) and he then came into the region about Jordan "preaching the baptism of repentance for the remission of sins." Along with this was the declaration that the kingdom of heaven was at hand, with the intimation that his ministry was to prepare the people spiritually to receive the Messiah. Had this been the only thrust of his message, clearly Jesus would not have been baptized, since He was sinless in both life and nature and hence had nothing of which to repent. Also He was Himself the Messiah. But the baptism of John had other implications also, and this led Jesus to offer Himself to John to be baptized.

111   What else was involved in John's baptism which caused Jesus to be baptized?

We learn from the gospel of John that one purpose of John the Baptist's mission was to make known who the Messiah was. According to John 1:33 the Baptist did not know Jesus was the Messiah until the time of the baptism. John undoubtedly knew who Jesus was as a person. They were related after the flesh (their mothers being cousins) according to Luke 1:36, though the word may not signify as close a relationship as is commonly thought. When Jesus came to be baptized John demurred and said he had need to be baptized by Jesus. He evidently had in mind the significance of repentance, and felt that Jesus was more holy than he. However, the Lord insisted, saying, "Thus it becometh us to fulfil all righteousness." He was not repenting of anything, but He was setting an example for others. For Himself there were a number of implications.

112   What were some of these?

The one which must have surprised John most was the fact of Jesus being marked out as the Messiah. John had been told by the One who commissioned him to baptize that when he saw the Holy Spirit descending and remaining on a person, that would be the Messiah, the One who should baptize with the Holy Spirit (Jn 1:33). The gospels record that as soon as Jesus was baptized and came up out of the water, the Holy Spirit descended upon Him in the form of a dove and remained upon Him (Lk 3:22). John forthwith states: "I saw, and bare record that this is the Son of God" (Jn 1:34). This is the first occasion since the birth of the Lord Jesus that He was marked out as the Son of God, the Messiah. This was not exactly a formal presentation of Him to the nation; that took place on the day we call Palm Sunday. But this was an announcement to those present that Jesus was the Son of God. This was confirmed by a voice from heaven saying, "Thou art my beloved Son, in whom I am well pleased." This incident is recorded in all three synoptic gospels—Matthew, Mark, and Luke.

Are there any other implications in Christ's baptism? 113

Yes, I think there is a symbolic significance also. In sharing in the baptism of those who were confessing their sins, desiring forgiveness, He was, in some sense, committting Himself to take their sins upon Himself in making atonement. The atonement had infinite value, and so was sufficient to put away the sins of the whole world, should they believe in Him. But in His baptism Christ was symbolically pledging Himself to die for our sins. His fulfilling all righteousness would be the public acknowledgment of the righteous requirement of God. He was not subject to it as they were who had sinned, but He submitted Himself to it as the One who would put away sin.

How does this relate to Christian baptism? 114

Only indirectly. It should be understood that John's baptism and that instituted by Christ after His resurrection carry a different significance. John's baptism is declared to be for repentance with a view to remission of sins, while Christian baptism is rather the confession of our faith in Christ. For this reason baptism is often joined with faith, but Scripture makes clear that it is not the immersion of the body in water which cleanses the soul, but the forgiveness of our sins by God in answer to our faith in Christ. The apostle Peter made this clear in the household of Cornelius when he said of Christ, "To him give all the prophets witness, that through his name whosoever believeth in him shall receive remission of sins" (Ac 10:43). The veracity of his message was confirmed by the Holy Spirit being given to the believing company while Peter preached. This was followed by their being baptized in water as a confession of their faith in this symbolic way.

The fact that baptism is in the name of the Father and of the Son and of the Holy Spirit indicates a relationship with each of the persons of the Trinity, which is the distinctive revelation of the New Testament. God always subsisted as a Trinity but the fact was not clearly understood. The Lord Jesus came to reveal the Father which included the fact that God is a Trinity. Many passages of Scripture amplify and clarify this. Our baptism is similar to that of Christ in that each is a symbolic act; but the symbolism is not precisely the same in both cases.

Could Jesus Have Sinned?

115 We are told in Hebrews 4:15 that Jesus was tempted in all points like as we are, yet without sin. Does this mean that He could have sinned, but didn't?

If we believe that Jesus was both God and man, He *could not* have sinned without involving and compromising His deity. We believe, therefore, that it was not possible for Him to have sinned. Scripture teaches plainly, in many passages, the absolute deity of Christ. One such passage is John 1:1-3: "In the beginning was the Word, and the Word was with God, and the Word was God. The same was in the beginning with God. All things were made by him, and without him was not anything made that was made." This is a clear statement that the Being called "the Word" was God and coeternal with the Father. It also makes clear that the Word had divine power and was, in fact, the actual Creator of all things. Verse 14 then states that "the Word was made flesh and dwelt among us, (and we beheld his glory, the glory as of the only begotten of the Father,) full of grace and truth." The next verse relates the testimony of John Baptist: "This was he of whom I spake, He that cometh after me is preferred before me: for he was before me." This positively identifies Jesus as the One called the Word. There can be no doubt of the deity of Christ, and this guarantees what is called His "impeccability," which means that He could not have sinned.

116 If this be so, how could it be said that He was tempted in all points like as we are?

We must not confuse temptation from without with response from within. He had presented to Him all the categories of temptation. First John 2:16 states: "All that is in the world, the lust of the flesh, and the lust of the eyes, and the pride of life, is not of the Father, but is of the world." That is to say, all temp-

tation to sin falls within these three categories; and the Lord
Jesus faced all three in His temptation in the wilderness at the
very beginning of His ministry. After fasting forty days it was
suggested to Him to change stones into bread both to satisfy His
hunger and to prove His deity. But He had taken upon Himself
the form of a servant and hence would do nothing except His
Father's will. It was also suggested that He cast Himself down
from the pinnacle of the temple so that the angels would bear
Him up and this would display His deity. But here again it would
have been a display of pride and would have "tempted" God.
Finally, He was shown all the kingdoms of the world and all the
glory of them in an appeal that He should worship Satan, who
would then give it all to Jesus. But the Lord Jesus not only
scorned this offer, He then commanded Satan to get behind Him,
for in resisting these three Christ had exhausted Satan's store-
house of temptation.

If Christ could not sin, does not this invalidate the temptations? 117

It is not the presentation of temptation from without which
constitutes sin, but response from within. Resistance to temptation does not invalidate the temptation, but it vindicates the person who resists. The fact that there was nothing in the Lord
Jesus to respond to sin in no way vitiates the actuality of the
temptation. When gold is given the acid test it is to prove that
it will not respond. If it were not pure, it would. The test is as
genuine as the gold. Before a newly constructed bridge is put
into general use, often it is tested by heavier weights than it is
expected to have to bear. The fact that the bridge stands such
a test raises no question of the reality of the test, but it establishes
the validity of the bridge as a public thoroughfare. A test is not
less valid because the subject passes the test.

How can Christ sympathize with us in our failures if He could 118 not have sinned?

While He did not experience failure in the sense of having any
deficiency in Himself, yet He was subjected to rejection. " He is
despised and rejected of men; a man of sorrows, and acquainted

with grief: and we hid as it were our faces from him; he was despised, and we esteemed him not" Isaiah tells us (53:3). Further, while He bore our griefs and carried our sorrows, "Yet we did esteem him stricken, smitten of God, and afflicted" (v. 4). Prophetically it is said of Him in Psalm 102:23-24, "He weakened my strength in the way; he shortened my days. I said, O my God, take me not away in the midst of my days." Isaiah 49:4 says, "Then I said, I have labored in vain, I have spent my strength for nought, and in vain: yet surely my judgment is with the LORD, and my work with my God." Acts 13:47 applies Isaiah 49 to the Lord Jesus, quoting from verse 6. At the end of His three and a half years of ministry the Lord Jesus had fewer disciples than Peter won on the day of Pentecost, and even His closest disciples forsook Him in the hour of His greatest trial.

Psalm 41:9 says: "Yea, mine own familiar friend, in whom I trusted, which did eat of my bread, hath lifted up his heel against me." When this was fulfilled by Judas, the Lord Jesus said: "Friend, wherefore art thou come?" (Mt 26:50). Psalm 69:20 says: "Reproach hath broken my heart; and I am full of heaviness: and I looked for some to take pity, but there was none; and for comforters, but I found none." So although the Lord Jesus had no element of deficiency in Himself, He knew the disappointments of His work not being accepted, and Himself being rejected.

119 In what sense was Christ "made perfect" through suffering? Does this imply previous imperfection?

This expression occurs more than once in the book of Hebrews. In chapter 2:10 we read: "For it became him, for whom are all things, and by whom are all things, in bringing many sons unto glory, to make the captain of their salvation perfect through sufferings." The word here translated "perfect" means to complete, or bring to maturity. There are many things which can only be known experientially. Hebrews 5:8-9 says: "Though he were a Son, yet learned he obedience by the things which he suffered; and being made perfect, he became the author of eternal salvation unto all them that obey him." This is amplified in 2:17-18: "Wherefore in all things it behoved him to be made like unto his brethren, that he might be a merciful and faithful high priest in things pertaining to God, to make reconciliation for the sins of the people. For in that he himself hath suffered being tempted, he is able to succor them that are tempted." There was no imperfection at any time, but the sufferings were very real, and accomplished the important purpose of enabling Him to be a merciful and faithful high priest for us. But this did not require that Christ should be able to sin, and we believe the other considerations show that this was not the case with Him.

How Is Christ's Birth of a Virgin Important to Christianity?

What is the importance to Christianity of Christ's being born of a virgin mother? 120

Scripture states it as a fact, both prophetically and historically, and if it were not so it would be a denial of the veracity and authority of the Bible. Besides, there are theological implications inherent in the fact of Christ's incarnation which make His birth of a virgin a necessity. A normal human birth would nullify much that is said of Him. The veracity of the Bible and the facts of Christ's deity, His birth of a virgin mother, and the circumstances of His atonement all stand or fall together. One cannot accept part of the record and deny other parts without becoming involved in hopeless contradictions.

Where in the Bible do we find reference to the fact that Christ was born of a virgin? 121

Historically it is found in the gospels of Matthew and Luke. These are the only ones which give us the details of Christ's birth, though there might be a more obscure reference to it in Galatians 4:4, where Paul speaks of Christ, God's Son, being made (or born) of a woman. The circumstances related in Matthew and Luke are precise and do not admit of any alternative interpretation; either we accept the record or we don't.

In the Old Testament perhaps the most precise statement of Christ's virgin birth is found in Isaiah 7:14-16: "Therefore the Lord himself shall give you a sign; Behold, a virgin shall conceive, and bear a son, and shall call his name Immanuel. Butter and honey shall he eat, that he may know to refuse the evil, and choose the good. For before the child shall know to refuse the evil, and choose the good, the land that thou abhorrest shall be forsaken of both her kings." The Hebrew word translated "virgin" can also mean, simply, maiden, and the context shows that the statement has a double application, since its immediate fulfillment constituted a sign to Ahaz, king of Judah. Yet it is equally clear that there is more in the text than the sign to Ahaz. Centuries later, when the Septuagint translation was made, the Greek word used to translate the Hebrew *alma* was *parthenos*, which designates specifically a virgin; and this is the word which Matthew uses when referring this prophecy to Christ's birth of Mary. The accounts of Matthew and Luke make it clear that no other interpretation can be put upon the application of this prophecy to the birth of Jesus, the Son of God.

122 Are there other scriptures which relate to this subject?

Yes. One that is taken by many to refer to Christ's birth of a virgin is Jeremiah 31:22: "The LORD hath created a new thing in the earth, A woman shall compass a man." If this has reference to Christ it would seem a clear statement that He was conceived in the womb of the virgin by the power of God. However many expositors do not believe this has any reference to Messiah, and we know of no New Testament passage to confirm it in that connection.

Perhaps the first reference in the Bible to the sending of Christ into the world is in Genesis 3:15, where there is the promise of the seed of the woman who should bruise the serpent's head (i.e., who should overcome the power of Satan). Normally genealogies are reckoned from the father. For example, in Hebrews 7:10 Levi is said to have been in the loins of Abraham when that patriarch paid tithes to Melchizedek. It is not said that he was in the womb of Sarah. Yet Genesis 3 speaks of the "seed of the woman." Hence Paul may have had Genesis 3:15 in mind when he wrote Galatians 4:4.

There is also the added fact that Christ is called "the second man" (1 Co 15:47). This indicates that His was not a normal birth since all between Adam and Christ were, in a sense, reproductions of Adam. With the birth of Christ we have One who was not generated from Adam. Luke 1:35 gives Gabriel's statement to Mary: "The Holy Ghost shall come upon thee, and the power of the Highest shall overshadow thee: therefore also that holy thing which shall be born of thee shall be called the Son of God."

How is Christian doctrine affected by this truth?   123

Had Christ been the product of human generation He would have had a sinful nature. It would have been utterly incongruous to combine deity with sinful humanity in one person. And besides, had it been so, He could not then have become our Saviour. He would have needed redemption Himself. Scripture does not teach that Christ took sinful human nature into His being, to lift it up to a higher plane by holy living. Rather, it teaches that He was sinless in His human life and nature because He was begotten in the womb of the virgin by the power of the Holy Spirit. He took our sins vicariously on the cross and paid the penalty in His atoning death and the shedding of His blood as the evidence of a life laid down sacrificially to meet the claims of the broken law. He lifts humanity first by putting away our sins and secondly by imparting His own eternal life to believers through the new birth. We are elevated in newness of life, not in our sinful condition.

How can we answer those who say Christians have imported this   124 teaching into their doctrine and that it is simply theological speculation?

There are those who even claim that Christians adopted the teaching of the virgin birth of Christ from the ancient religion of Babylon! The truth is rather the reverse. In many places in the Bible we are told that God planned both creation and redemption before anything was created. Such passages as 1 Peter 1:18-20, Revelation 13:8 and 17:8 show clearly that God's pur-

poses regarding redemption were not an afterthought, brought
in to cover an unforeseen contingency. There was divine foreknowledge and appointment. However God's planning does not
eliminate the development in experience of the things He has
foreseen and foreknown. Nor does He prematurely reveal what
His plans are, except in a limited degree, to those who are believers. His revelation of Himself and His truth to men is on a
progressive basis. There is reason to believe that God revealed
many things to those who trusted Him in the early days of human
experience, even before the Bible came into being. The ancient
pagan religions were therefore corruptions of the pure revelation
of God, as many today corrupt the truths revealed in the Bible.
Let us be sure we are not among the number who do that, but let
us rather trust and obey the eternal truths revealed to us in the
written Word of God, the holy Bible.

What Is Known of the Family Life of Christ?

**125 Are there any nonbiblical sources of information about the life
of Christ, and if so, are they reliable?**

All that is known *authentically* about the life of Christ is what
is found in the Bible. The Schaff-Herzog *Encyclopedia of Religious Knowledge* points out that while there are numerous works
which mention Him, such references are more in the nature of an
accreditation of the spiritual vigor of Christianity than a genuine
source of information about its Founder. It wasn't until after the
death of Christ that the importance of His life was realized. The
so-called Hebrew Gospel contains "a profusion of historical in-
ventions" which brand it as unreliable, while the later apocryphal
gospels "were fantastic attempts to fill up the gaps in the life of
our Lord, especially in the periods of His infancy, childhood, and
passion, and are only valuable for the contrast they present to the
canonical Gospels" (ibid.). A passage in Josephus often referred
to is considered spurious, at least in its present form. Yet the
fact that the reference occurs in all the manuscripts and is noted

by Eusebius, the early Church historian, gives ground for assuming there may have been a genuine favorable reference to Christ by Josephus.

How do the gospels deal with the life of Christ, especially His birth and childhood? 126

Only two of the gospels give us an account of the birth of Christ, each of them including a genealogy. Matthew starts with Abraham and comes down to "Joseph the husband of Mary, of whom [fem. sing.] was born Jesus, who is called Christ" (1:16). Luke begins with Jesus and traces the genealogy back to Adam. Many believe Luke's statement that Joseph was the "son" of Heli (2:23) means simply that he was his son by marriage. In the original language the word *son* does not occur in the entire list and was supplied by the translators to make better reading in the English text. Hence some would read that Joseph was son-in-law of Heli, making Heli *Mary's* father, which is probably the case.

Both Matthew and Luke give one or two incidents in the babyhood of Jesus. Luke also tells of Jesus' going with Joseph and Mary to Jerusalem when He was twelve years of age. We are told nothing of the visit until the parents left on their return journey, when Jesus remained behind in Jerusalem. His absence from the company was not discovered at once, as Joseph and Mary assumed He was somewhere in the traveling party. After a search of three days He was found in the temple, engaged in conversation with the priests. Following this we are told that "He went down with them, and came to Nazareth, and was subject unto them" (Lk 2:51). All that is said of Him concerning the years that intervened until, at the age of thirty, He made His appearance to the public is: "And Jesus increased in wisdom and stature, and in favor with God and man" (v. 52).

What is the significance of Christ's genealogy and early life? 127

The record shows Him to have been descended from Abraham and David, thus fulfilling the Messianic promises made to these patriarchs. He was born of a virgin mother, both fulfilling prophecy and also meeting all that was involved in the incarnation of the Son of God. Luke, himself a physician, gives many intimate details about Christ's birth. Matthew includes an incident which many consider to have taken place a year or more after Christ's birth, since after the visit of the Magi Herod had all the children of Bethlehem killed who were "two years old and under" (2:16). Matthew also records the flight into Egypt to escape this holocaust and the subsequent settlement of the family in Nazareth. Luke reveals that Nazareth had been the home of Mary and Joseph prior to the birth of Christ.

128 What is told us in the Bible about Joseph and about the brothers of Jesus?

In Luke 2:48 Mary calls Joseph the father of Jesus, but this evidently refers to his place in the household and is not intended to refute Matthew and Luke's accounts of Christ's birth of her as a virgin. Joseph is not mentioned again in the Bible after the incident in Luke 2, and many believe he died before our Lord's public ministry. This is suggested by the fact that some, who had known Joseph, referred to Jesus as "the carpenter's son" (Mt 13:55), while others called Him "the carpenter, the son of Mary" (Mk 6:3). It is in this context that the names of the brothers of Jesus are listed: James and Joses, Juda and Simon. Some argue that these were cousins, but they are included in the household as part of the family. Also, the people added, "And are not his sisters here with us?" Female cousins would not be referred to in this way.

Some have argued that if He had had brothers, Jesus would not have committed His mother to the care of John the disciple (Jn 19:26-27). But we are told in John 7 that His brothers did not at that time accept the Lord's claims to be the Messiah, which could well account for this transfer of responsibility. Some of them at least, if not all, did believe on Him later, and it may be that the Holy Spirit used this incident to help arouse their consciences in this respect. One of Christ's brothers became a leader in the Jerusalem church (Ac 15), and it is he who wrote the epistle of James. Many also believe the epistle of Jude was written by another brother. The argument that these "brothers" were sons of Joseph by a former marriage will not stand up, since in that case the oldest son of Joseph would have inherited the title to David's throne, and he also would have been the protector of Mary, Joseph's widow. Both these fell on the Lord Jesus, Joseph's oldest legal son, even though Joseph was not his actual father.

What are the most important events in the life of Christ?   129

It is difficult to make comparisons in importance, but we suggest that perhaps the two most important points in the life of Christ are His incarnation (taking human life into His being, apart from sin) and His atonement, when He accomplished the purpose of His incarnation and put away sin by the sacrifice of Himself (Heb 9:26). In His life on earth He demonstrated perfectly how God intended man to live, and He illustrated, as well as expounded, the meaning of God's laws. In this He left an example for those who believe in Him, that we should follow His steps (1 Pe 2:21). However it is a fatal mistake to think that this is what takes us to heaven, for no human being, sharing Adam's fallen, sinful nature, could possibly follow perfectly in the steps of Jesus. Yet James 2:10 shows that if we are to be accepted by God on the ground of our own lives and characters, God demands absolute perfection. A single sin would shut us out of heaven. It is highly important to realize that all that is said of our good works relates to time subsequent to our conversion to Christ and does not precede it.

Why Was Jesus Called the Son of Man?

What is the meaning of the term "Son of man," found in both Old 130
and New Testaments?

This was a term commonly used for man, although its significance varies according to its use in a particular context. Ellicott's Commentary has a helpful note on the use of the term in Ezekiel 2:2: " 'Son of man' for 'man' is so common in the Aramaic languages that it is even used for Adam himself in the Syriac version of I Corinthians 15:45-47." The term is usually used of man in general, though in Psalm 8:4 it may imply generation: "What is man, that thou art mindful of him? and the son of man, that thou visitest him?" Looking back to Adam, even in his sinless state he was an infinitesimal part of God's vast creation. But the use of "son of man" in that context seems to imply that Adam's offspring inherited his sinful nature and hence were even less worthy of God's consideration. But the ordinary use of the term conveys the simple thought of manhood.

131 Is the term used of individuals?

In Daniel 8:17 the angel Gabriel used the term in addressing Daniel: "Understand, O son of man: for at the time of the end shall be the vision." And the term is used about 90 times with reference to the prophet Ezekiel. In these usages there seems to be a recognition of the frailty of Ezekiel and Daniel as human beings. We know of no reason to think that the term was used to set apart these two prophets as having a special place in the counsels of God. Both of them were part of the captivity in Babylon, where the phrase was a common one, and it seems to indicate that God recognized their dependent state and was assuring them of His divine empowerment to enable them to fulfill His purposes.

132 If the term implies the frailty of man, why was it used of Christ?

This usage has its roots in an Old Testament reference (Dan 7:13), which speaks of "one like the Son of man" who "came with the clouds of heaven, and came to the Ancient of days." We are told that "the prominence which the Maccabean struggles gave to the predictions of Daniel drew attention to the name as it had thus been used. The 'Son of man' became one of the titles of the expected Christ. The Targum or Paraphrase of the Psalms (probably earlier than our Lord's ministry) explains even such a passage as Psalm 80:17 ('the son of man whom thou madest so strong for thine own self') as referring to Christ" (Ellicott). In this context the term would have a different significance from the other references mentioned, and the use of it would, in a certain sense, constitute a claim to Messiahship.

How is the term used in the New Testament?

It seems significant that in the New Testament the term is used only *of* Christ—and only *by* Christ with very few exceptions. One of these was when Stephen was about to be stoned, and we read that "He, being full of the Holy Ghost, looked up steadfastly into heaven, and saw the glory of God, and Jesus standing on the right hand of God, and said, Behold, I see the heavens opened, and the Son of man standing on the right hand of God" (Ac 7:55-56). Also, when John was describing the revelation to him of Christ in glory, he said that he saw "in the midst of the seven candlesticks one like unto the Son of man" (Rev 2:13); and he went on to describe His appearance. And in Revelation 14:14, describing another vision, John said, "I looked, and behold a white cloud, and upon the cloud one sat like unto the Son of man."

The term does not occur at all in the epistles, and in the gospel records it is always used by the Lord except on one occasion when the crowd repeated it, reacting to His use of it. Their query showed that they considered it a Messianic title but were mystified with regard to one or two aspects of His use of it. "The people answered him, We have heard out of the law that Christ [Messiah] abideth forever: and how sayest thou, The Son of man must be lifted up? who is this Son of man?" (Jn 12:34). Their problem seems to be twofold: How does what you say fit in with Messianic prophecy, and also, who are you to speak as though these things apply to you? They were not ready to accept Jesus as the Christ, and they could not reconcile what He said with their already conceived notions of what the Messiah would be like when He should come.

What reasons can be given for our Lord's adopting this title?

First of all it should be noticed that the term is always used in a generic sense (*anthropos*) and never as son of a particular man (*aneer*). While the Lord Jesus, in His incarnation, partook of true humanity, it was without taint of sin. He was begotten in the womb of the virgin by the divine power of the Holy Spirit and so did not partake of Adam's sinful nature, though born of a woman and possessing true humanity. He is therefore called "the second man" (1 Co 15:47). All who came in between were simply reproductions of Adam. And as the head of a new race (in redemption) Christ is called "the last Adam" (v. 45).

However, while maintaining these safeguards with regard to the purity of His life and nature, the term was a recognition that He had come into manhood and had made it part of His being, so that even in resurrection He is called both man and Son of man. In 1 Timothy 2:5-6 we read: "There is one God, and one mediator between God and men, the man Christ Jesus; who gave himself a ransom for all, to be testified in due time." His use of the term therefore betokens His entering into actual manhood (apart from sin) and links His humanity with His deity.

Also, in view of its Messianic association in Daniel 7, the term constitutes a claim to be the Messiah. In Matthew 13:41 the millennial kingdom is said to be that of the Son of man. This gives New Testament verification for the Messianic interpretation of Daniel 7. One commentary considers the use of the term *Son of man* to be perhaps the chief connecting link between the teaching of the first three gospels and that of the fourth.

It is of interest to note that the expression is not found in any of the epistles and that it never found its way into the theological or liturgical phraseology of the Church. This reserve has helped to preserve the use of the term from degenerating into something derogatory to the uniqueness of Christ's manhood. It expresses infinite grace linked with divine glory.

Was Jesus a Revolutionary?

135 Does the Bible represent Jesus as a revolutionary, as many persons claim?

Not in the modern sense of the word. That Jesus did revolutionize the lives of many persons is true. And that Christianity did, for a time, make a revolutionary impact on the world is equally true. But we are speaking of moral and spiritual revolution, not political. One of the accusations against the Lord Jesus was that He made Himself a king. But when Pilate asked Him if He were a king, Jesus replied, "My kingdom is not of this world: if my kingdom were of this world, then would my servants fight, that I should not be delivered to the Jews: but now is my kingdom not from hence" (Jn 18:36). At one point the people would have made Him a king by force, but He eluded them (Jn 6:15). They would have welcomed a political revolutionary, but this was not His mission. The disciples were charged with turning the world upside down (Ac 17:6). The Berkeley version uses the term "these world revolutionists," but it should be noted that this charge was made by their enemies, and it is not defined. If they meant that the disciples engaged in political revolution, the charge was completely unfounded.

Was it an act of violence or revolution when Jesus entered the temple and drove out the money changers with a scourge? 136

No, it was not. This incident is often misunderstood and misrepresented. This was not at all in the nature of a political action. It had to do with the temple, the house of God. The Lord Jesus did not inaugurate a movement, but acted individually. He was not rebelling against the constituted authority of the time, though that was far from just and was soon to condemn Him to death. He was there as Son over God's house (Heb 3:6), and what He condemned was the abuse of the house of God. They had made it a house of merchandise (Jn 2:16) and a den of thieves (Mt 21:13). He did not inaugurate a movement against the authority of the high priest, but He drove out of the temple those who were desecrating the sanctity of that building by using the premises as a mart for the selling of animals and birds for sacrifice. It was not only the fact that the character of the place was changed from that of prayer and worship to that of commerce, but the presence of live animals and birds would defile the sanctuary by their dirt.

Jesus also drove out the money changers who took advantage of the fact that on certain feast days all the males of Israel were required to attend the ritual in Jerusalem. Since the nation had been dispersed, men came from various parts of the empire. This required the changing of their money into local currency. But what was inaugurated as a convenience became a racket, and exorbitant fees were charged for this service. We have no record of Jesus trying to stop currency exchange. He merely drove the money changers out of the temple because their dishonesty defiled it.

137   Was not the scourging of them a violent protest?

In a sense, but not as we understand violence today. The
scourge He used was not the cruel type used in the official flog-
ging of prisoners. Those were made of leather, knotted, with bits
of bone or metal fastened in the knots so that they cut and lacer-
ated the skin, reducing one's back to a mass of bleeding flesh.
Scripture says the Lord Jesus made a scourge of "small cords"
(Jn 2:15), with no suggestion of inflicting serious injury. It was
rather a means of enforcing compliance with His demand that
they clear out of the temple, which He called His Father's house.
To equate this with rock throwing and other forms of violence and
destruction does not fairly represent what the Bible says. Neither
was it a mass demonstration. He acted in His individual right as
the incarnate Son of God.

**138   Do such actions invalidate the description of Him as "meek and
lowly"?**

No, they do not. It was the Lord Jesus Christ Himself who
said, "Take my yoke upon you, and learn of me; for I am meek
and lowly in heart: and ye shall find rest unto your souls" (Mt
11:29). Because these terms have been included in certain
hymns, some have the mistaken notion that they originated in a
human assessment of Christ. Some have tried to reverse this, and
describe the Lord Jesus in earthy terms which He Himself rejected. He stands in contrast with men like Barabbas, "who for
a certain sedition [insurrection] made in the city, and for murder,
was cast into prison" (Lk 23:19). Many in that day looked for,
and desired, one who would move by violence to throw off the
yoke of Rome. The Lord Jesus neither moved in this direction
Himself, nor did He ever encourage others to do so.

It is significant, too, that He never sought improvement in His
own circumstances. He would rebuke others for desecrating God's
house, and He met the needs of the poor and sick contrary to the
ideas of the leaders. But He did not start a movement to over-
throw the existing order of things. Rather, He instructed His followers in such a way that their own lives were changed. He reminded men of God's claims and standards with the warning that

their entire life would come into review before Him who without respect of persons judges every man. His type of revolution was successful because His followers did not wait for society to change. Their lives were changed and eventually this had the effect of changing society.

Did not Moses, and the three young Hebrews, and others in the 139 Old Testament demonstrate against the authority in power?

The circumstances were quite different. Moses was divinely appointed and was a man of faith and submission to God. It appears that his earlier attempt to deliver his Israelitish brethren was premature, and more in the nature of present-day violence. God did not sustain him in that. Moses fled into the wilderness and for forty years learned to know more of God. He lost his self-confidence and reentered Egypt by the call and commission of God. Israel was a nation of destiny, both by promise and prophecy. Moses, chosen by God to be its leader and deliverer, was a man of God, and the meekest man in all the earth (Num 12:3). He did not act in self-assertion, nor from national pride, but in subjection to the will of God and in the power of the Spirit of God. When Pharaoh rejected the demands made upon him, it was God who retaliated and sent plagues. The whole experience was a divine manifestation.

The case of the three young Hebrews was different, though, as with Moses, there was no organized rebellion or violence. The king demanded the worship of an idol. These young men were believers in Jehovah, the living and true God. They refused to bow down to an idol, since that would violate the second of the Ten Commandments. They risked their lives in this refusal, but they neither threatened nor molested anyone. They simply refused to disobey God, and were prepared to take the consequences (Dan 3:17-18). This is quite different from a revolutionary movement, perhaps organized by men who do not acknowledge Christ's lordship over them, who yet demand the cooperation of Christians on the plea that this is practical Christianity. We do not see that the Lord Jesus, nor the others mentioned, ever set such a pattern.

DEATH

Does the Bible Teach That Man Is Immortal?

140 Does the Bible teach that man is immortal, or is this an importation from the ancient philosophers?

Many Bible passages speak of a life beyond the death of the body and of the resurrection of all mankind. Scripture speaks of those who have died as having continued conscious existence in a spirit world and indicates that they have identifiable personalities capable of experiencing comfort or pain. Some have contended that this is a carryover from Greek philosophy, but even the early books of the Bible, which antedate the writings of the Greeks, refer to it; and in the New Testament both the Lord Jesus Christ and the various writers speak of it.

One such discussion is reported in Matthew 22 and Luke 20, where certain of the sect of the Sadducees questioned the validity of this concept. They did not believe in resurrection, nor in angels or spirits (Ac 23:8), and they sought to confound Christ by raising a suppositious case in connection with the law of levirate marriage. They told of seven brothers, one of whom married and died childless. According to this law, the next brother then married the widow, but he also died childless. Each then married her in turn, but each died without children; and finally the woman died. Their question was, "Whose shall she be in the resurrection?" To them, this was unanswerable.

The Lord Jesus' comment was: "Ye do err, not knowing the scriptures, nor the power of God" (Mt 22:29); and He went on to explain that marriage has to do with life here on earth and that there will be no marriage in heaven. He also referred to the resurrection but included conscious life in the interval between death and resurrection. He pointed out that Moses at the burning bush had called the Lord the God of Abraham, of Isaac, and of Jacob, and He added: "For he is not a God of the dead, but of the living: for all live unto him" (Lk 20:38). These patriarchs not only will be raised but in the meantime are alive. God is not the God of the dead.

Does the Genesis record of creation speak of man as being immortal? 141

Not by using that term, but it shows plainly that the creation of man included an impartation of life from God in a different way than the rest of creation. The material universe was created by the word of His power: "He spake, and it was done; he commanded, and it stood fast" (Ps 33:9). So it was also with the lower forms of animate creatures. God said, "Let the waters bring forth abundantly the moving creature that hath life, and fowl that may fly above the earth in the open firmament of heaven" (Gen 1:20). And again, "Let the earth bring forth the living creature after his kind, cattle, and creeping thing, and beast of the earth after his kind: and it was so" (v. 24). Animal life, like the material universe, was brought into being by the word of His power.

The creation of man was quite distinct. Of him alone it is said, "Let us make man in our image, after our likeness" (v. 26). No other creature is said to be made in the likeness of God. Nor was man formed simply by God's spoken word. Genesis 2:7 tells us that God "formed man of the dust of the ground, and breathed into his nostrils the breath of life; and man became a living soul." There was a direct impartation from God which made man "a living soul." Nothing is said here of man's spirit, but later scriptures show that when God breathed into man, He imparted to him a spirit which gave man a different kind of life from that of the beasts. We are told in 2 Peter 2:12 that brute beasts (or irrational animals) were "made to be taken and destroyed." This does not condone torturing them, but it shows they are not immortal, and it justifies using their flesh for food, as other scriptures teach.

142 Is the doctrine of man's immortality important to Christianity?

Definitely. And perhaps we should point out that the term "immortality," as applied in the Bible to men, refers to the body. The immortality of the soul, while taught specifically in such passages as those to which we have already referred in Matthew 22 and Luke 20, is assumed and implied in many others. Death is not cessation of being. Physical death is the separation of spirit and soul from the body. "The body without the spirit is dead," says James (2:26). Spiritual death is the separation of man from God. "You hath be quickened, who were dead in trespasses and sins" (Eph 2:1). We were physically alive but spiritually dead, because we were separated from God. The second death (Rev 20:14) does not mean a second physical death but rather eternal separation from God.

The importance of this doctrine lies in the fact that there is in life a law of recompense or retribution. But this law does not always operate within the limits of one's life on earth, nor is it intended that it should. Part of the life of faith is the fact that we believe there is a living God and a spirit world and a life beyond our physical life here on earth. Christ taught that no one receives a full recompense in this life, for either good or evil. We may receive a partial recompense, but His own experience, and that of the martyrs and of many others, shows that one may suffer the loss of all things in doing the will of God without recompense in this world. Likewise many persons throughout history lived in sin and in violent oppression of others without any apparent retribution.

But there is a significant proposition in 1 Timothy 5:24-25, "Some men's sins are open beforehand, going before to judgment; and some men they follow after. Likewise also the good works of some are manifest beforehand; and they that are otherwise can not be hid." Were there no existence beyond physical death, life would have no essential meaning, and there would be no refutation of either of two false philosophies. One is: "Let us eat, drink, and be merry, for tomorrow we die." There would be no valid argument against hedonism if there were no life beyond physical death. Nor would there be against the ribald philosophy, "Let dog eat dog, and the devil take the hindmost." The chief end of life would be self-gratification, whether in pleasure or in power. The Christian philosophy teaches man's accountability to God and the need for cleansing from sin. It also teaches that in personal salvation there is a new birth, wherein the love of God is shed abroad in our hearts by the Holy Spirit, who is given to us, enabling and causing us to love our fellowmen. And it promises recompense in the world to come for a life lived for the glory of God and divine retribution to those who live and die in their sins. Man's immortality is an essential part of the Christian faith.

What Happens to Infants Who Die?

Are children who die before reaching an age of accountability 143 considered "innocent" in the eyes of God? If so, do they go to heaven?

Let us consider the first question first: "Are children who die before reaching an age of accountability considered 'innocent' in the eyes of God?" The answer is no. Only three persons came into the world without sin. Two might be termed innocent. The third is said to be holy. An innocent person is one who is undefiled but who may be drawn into sin. A truly holy person is sin-resistant. The Lord Jesus Christ was both God and man and was not susceptible to sinning. Adam and Eve were created without sin but before long were drawn into it.

With regard to the offspring of Adam and Eve, we are all born with a sinful nature. The apostle Paul wrote in Ephesians 2:3 that we "were by nature children of wrath, even as others." An apple tree is not an apple tree because it bears apples. It was an apple tree before it bore apples, and it bears apples because it *is* an apple tree. It would be an apple tree if it never bore apples. There are flowering varieties which do not bear fruit, yet have the nature of an apple tree, and their shape and leaves and bark and various features bear witness to their identity. Similarly we sin because we have a sinful nature, derived from sinful antecedent life. It all began when Adam and Eve became sinners and then begat offspring in their likeness (Gen 5:3). After Adam and Eve sinned there never was another innocent person. The Lord Jesus, as we have said, was holy (Lk 1:35). No one will be in heaven on the ground of innocency.

144 Does this mean that infants who die are lost?

Far from it, although Scripture does not make any direct statement about the matter, so far as I know. But it does teach inferentially, I believe, that those who die before reaching accountability are taken to heaven. A statement of our Lord often quoted in this connection is found in Matthew 19:14: "Suffer little children, and forbid them not, to come unto me: for of such is the kingdom of heaven." This does not mean that children are born saved and later become lost, but rather that, though born lost, they go to heaven at death if they have not reached accountability. This seems to be confirmed by comparing Luke 19:10 with Matthew 18:11. The passage in Luke, having reference to adults, says, "For the Son of man is come to seek and to save that which was lost." Referring to little children, Matthew says, "For the Son of man is come to save that which was lost." The omission of "seek" from the text in Matthew seems to imply that children who die in infancy are automatically saved through the blood of Christ. 1 John 2:2 shows that Christ made propitiation for the sins of the whole world, and while adults must receive Him in faith in order to be saved, it appears that God credits the saving power of Christ's atonement to little children whom He takes to Himself. Some think David was expressing his confidence in this in 2 Samuel 12:23, but others consider that he was merely referring to the fact of death.

145 Does the Bible teach that a child must be baptized in order to go to heaven?

We believe not. Christians differ widely in their understanding of the meaning and purpose of baptism, but in my understanding of the Bible it is the public confession of our faith in Christ. In no reference to baptism in the Bible do I see anything that makes it part of our salvation. Our relationship to God is a purely spiritual one, expressed in physical acts and forms but not dependent on them. We believe this is true for both adults and children.

Another consideration is the fact that if the salvation of a child depended on its being baptized, it would mean that the eternal destiny and experience of the child would be dependent on a physical act performed by another on its behalf. This does not seem to me to represent the truth of the gospel. For God to give His Son to bear the sin of the world and put it away by the sacrifice of Himself and then permit a child to be lost forever because someone did not baptize him seems incongruous.

Does the Bible make any distinction between a child of Christian 146 parents and one of heathen origin or one who is born to unbelievers?

I do not see any distinction in this regard. All are sinners because they are related to Adam. Those who are saved are accepted by God because of their relationship to Christ; their acceptance does not rest on their relationship to some other human being. Christian grace, and particularly salvation, is not transmitted by natural birth, nor is it acquired by family association. Christ died for all, and when the Lord Jesus speaks of "little children" we do not see any suggestion that some receive favorable treatment while others do not. This may help to explain why God has allowed infant mortality to be high in heathen lands. All these infants who have died have gone to heaven, in the wisdom and providence of God. What we learn in eternity may alter many of the judgments we form now, and the believer can safely trust God to do what is right and best.

What will be the state of children in heaven? Will they remain 147 as infants or develop there?

Many have advanced the theory of development—both physical and mental—in heaven. This idea grows out of the concept of heaven as a projection of earth. But we do not believe this is a valid concept. Conditions in heaven will be entirely different.

On the other hand, neither do we believe that there will be infancy in heaven. If there were infants in heaven, then there should also be something similar at the opposite end of the spectrum, and we would find old people, physically decrepit and perhaps deformed. But Scripture speaks of our having new bodies in heaven, suited to the conditions there. We do not believe there will be a continuation of any kind of defect or deformity. We understand the Bible to teach that we shall be like Christ (1 Jn 3:1-3) and that our bodies will be in a glorified state, which will be the perfection of new creation. If one who has reached senility on earth can be brought back to the vigor of youth, we see no reason why one who has died in infancy cannot be advanced to maturity of body and mind. This will certainly have to be accomplished for those who are illiterate and deformed and undeveloped; and we believe it will be accomplished for all who are received into heaven. All will be there in the full vigor of life, both body and mind, in a glorified state.

Is It Biblical to Honor the Dead?

148 Is it biblical to honor dead persons, or is this a pagan custom?

Usually the Bible speaks of giving honor to living persons to whom it is due, though we know of no condemnation of memorializing the dead. The Bible does teach, by example, that we should show respect for the *bodies* of those who have died. In the early chapters of Genesis we have an account of the deaths of numerous patriarchs, but nothing is said of the disposal of their bodies. The first mention of burial (Gen 15:15) refers to it in a casual way, indicating that this was the customary way of disposing of the bodies of the dead. In Genesis 23 we have a detailed account of how Abraham acquired a burying place for Sarah, and in 49:29-31 we are told that this became the family burying plot. Meantime Rachel, Jacob's beloved wife, had died near Bethlehem. She was buried there, and Jacob erected a pillar or monument to mark the spot (35:19-20). Since erecting pillars with inscriptions to mark certain places and commemorate certain events was common (28:18; 31:45; 35:14), the marker for Rachel's grave was a natural thing. In the New Testament one of the words for sepulcher signifies a memorial and suggests a monument or marker of some kind.

Does burial have any special significance?   149

We understand there are two reasons for giving honorable burial to those who have died. One is the recognition of the fact that the body is part of the person and is not to be desecrated. The other is that we believe in the resurrection of the dead, and one of the figures of resurrection in the New Testament is the planting of a seed and its resurrection in newness of life. Thus the "planting" of the body indicates the anticipation of its resurrection. However the Bible does not *command* burial, and the wisdom of this is apparent, since in many cases burial would be impossible. Some persons die at sea. Others perish in a wilderness, perhaps being devoured by wild beasts. Many martyrs were burned at the stake. Had the Bible commanded burial there might have been some distress of mind on the part of the families of such persons. Others, for various reasons, decide to will their bodies for scientific use or donate eyes or other parts of their bodies for transplanting to others. The Bible does not require burial, though it is taught by example.

Some people object to monuments or other memorials on the ground that it is a waste of money that could be utilized to better advantage. Is this a valid objection?   150

In some cases, where elaborate memorials are erected, it may indeed be a waste of money that could be used more advantageously, though often persons erecting such memorials would not use the money for the work of the gospel anyway. A modest memorial can hardly be objected to on economic grounds, since we spend money for various esthetic purposes. As with anything else, one must use wisdom in deciding what type of memorial, if any, should be used. Wealthy persons often erect elaborate memorials, though in many modern cemeteries, there are rules limiting memorials to a simple bronze plaque, placed on a low granite stone to mark the grave. The value of elaborate memorials is questionable, since most are ignored with the passing of time.

151 **What about holding memorial services, especially for those who have died long ago? Is this proper in the light of the Bible?**

We see no objection to memorializing the dead if this is done on a proper basis. On the highest plane, we memoralize the death of Christ in the holy communion supper, observed by the Church throughout its history in keeping with the Lord's command when He instituted it immediately preceding His death. The commemoration of Christ's death is not merely historic but deeply spiritual, and His death is the basis of our acceptance with God. It has eternal significance of the deepest import.

On the human scale we see no objection to giving recognition to the heroic acts and lives of those who have preceded us, especially where these have secured to us the liberties we enjoy under God. Scripture tells us we are to "render . . . to all their dues: tribute to whom tribute is due; custom to whom custom; fear to whom fear; honor to whom honor" (Rom 13:7). In such commemoration we are reminded of the cost of our privileges, and this should inculcate in us a greater appreciation for them and a determination to be worthy of them and to preserve them. However we must keep in mind that men may have been heroic in a political or military or social sense and yet not be persons we should emulate in spiritual matters.

152 **Is there any other kind of memorial besides erecting monuments and holding services where the deeds and exploits of those we honor are given recognition?**

A far more significant monument is to prove ourselves worthy of our heritage and to be willing to accept the disciplines involved in preserving the liberties and benefits which they have secured for us. Men seldom acknowledge any indebtedness for privileges they do not value. History shows that many times men and nations have lost liberties by neglect of the conditions which make them possible. Abuse of privilege and neglect of responsibility combine to make possible the loss of privileges considered inherent in life because they were procured by preceding generations. The cost of maintaining a free society differs from the cost of obtaining our liberties, but there is a price to be paid in self-discipline, which, if it is not accepted, can easily result in the loss of the way of life we so much cherish.

Spiritually, while the Lord's Supper was instituted by Jesus Christ Himself as a perpetual memorial of Him and His atoning death on our behalf, even this can become an empty form unless there is also the memorial of a life lived in obedience to His teaching and devoted to His service. The importance of a living memorial, in contrast with one of stone is emphasized in 2 Corinthians 3:3-11. Paul speaks of an epistle commending Christ to the world, "written not with ink, but with the Spirit of the living God; not in tables of stone, but in fleshy tables of the heart." The latter, he says, is far more glorious than the former. So let us honor Christ by life and lip, by word and work, as well as in the forms and liturgies of church services.

Is Reincarnation a Biblical Concept?

What is meant by the term "reincarnation," and where did the **153** **idea originate?**

Reincarnation is also called metempsychosis, or the transmigration of souls. It refers to the teaching that at death, or at some point of time thereafter, the soul of a human being reenters life in another body. This may be in another human body, or in some cases it is taught that the soul may enter the body of an animal, or even an insect. This teaching is believed to have been current in ancient Egypt, and the idea is found also in Hinduism and Buddhism, as well as being held by some other groups.

It appears to have been the outgrowth of an attempt to relate human immortality to a condition where there is no personal supreme being, to whom we give account of our lives, though the teaching in this respect is somewhat varied and imprecise. The Bible teaches that men once knew God, and later turned away from Him, leading to spiritual confusion. We read: "Because that, when they knew God, they glorified him not as God, neither were thankful; but became vain in their imaginations, and their foolish heart was darkened" (Ro 1:21). The passage goes on to relate how men then became idolaters, and "changed the glory of the incorruptible God into an image made like to corruptible man . . . and four-footed beasts, and creeping things" (v. 23). In the wake of giving divine dignity to a variety of creatures, it was easy to think of the soul of someone who had died entering into them.

154 What relationship, if any, does one's character have to his subsequent life, according to these teachings?

Usually it is held that one's conduct in one life cycle determines his status in the next. Some religions teach that there is first a temporary period of reward or punishment, and then one returns to a life appropriate to the character he had formed in his previous existence. The Encyclopaedia Britannica says that the idea of the transmigration of souls is fundamental to most philosophies and religions of India, though the earliest Aryan scripture, the Rigveda (early first millennium B.C.) does not teach it. It is said that the first formulated doctrine came into being about 600 B.C. It teaches that the life cycle can be broken only when one develops a character which permits assimilation into the Absolute, or Brahmin. Buddhism is somewhat similar, though the Encyclopaedia says this religion denies "an unchanging or substantial soul." But it is believed that a "germ of consciousness" passes into the womb of a mother, and the nature of the new individual will depend on "the quality of the potencies (karma) contained within the germ." Only by stopping karma, "all the desires or 'cravings' founded upon the illusion of a permanent, immutable self," can one reach Nirvana, "a state of eternal bliss."

155 How does this relate to the teaching of the Bible with regard to the life after death?

It is a contradiction of the Bible teaching except for the fact of continued existence after death; and even that fact is perverted. It is interesting to note that such teaching is not found in early Jewish literature. The Jewish nation had a divinely given revelation, which kept them from many gross distortions of truth. In cases where, through over-literalism in interpreting Bible teaching, they looked for a reappearance on earth of Elijah, or any other biblical character, it was not in the sense of their being reincarnated in someone else, but rather a restoration to life of the person himself. We are not aware of their ever holding to a mingling of personalities, much less of a human being later becoming subhuman. Some religious philosophies encouraged the thought that a flower, blooming out of the grave of a dead person, contained the soul of that person.

How does the Bible contradict the thought of reincarnation, whether in another human life, or in some beast, or bird, or insect? 156

With regard to any subhuman form of existence, this would deny the biblical teaching that man is a special creation of God, made in His image, in a way that is true of no other creature. In the record of creation we read only of man that there was a divine consultation before bringing him into being. "And God said, Let us make man in our image, after our likeness: and let them have dominion over the fish of the sea, and over the fowl of the air, and over cattle, and over all the earth, and over every creeping thing that creepeth upon the earth" (Gen 1:26). And in the act of creating man, "The Lord God . . . breathed into his nostrils the breath of life; and man became a living soul" (Gen 2:7). Of no other creature do we read of any such direct impartation from God, and all the references to man show that he has a distinctive place in creation. He has special privileges and responsibilities, and it would not be possible for his spirit to inhabit any lower form of life. Reincarnation of a human being in a lower form of life would deny man's distinctive place in creation.

How does this contradict the thought of man being reincarnated as another human being? 157

Scripture not only teaches that man is a distinctive order of creation, but that each person is a distinctive personality, with an indestructible soul. The Lord Jesus said, "Fear not them which kill the body, but are not able to kill the soul: but rather fear him which is able to destroy both soul and body in hell" (Mt 10:28). In fact, the Bible teaches that even our bodies will be raised at a future time (Jn 5:28-29). This guarantees the indestructibility of personality, and thus makes impossible the transmigration of the soul of anyone into another person or form of life.

This is emphasized and enforced by the teaching of man's accountability to God. "It is appointed unto men once to die, and after this the judgment," we read in Hebrews 9:27. Romans 14:12 says, "So then every one of us shall give account of himself to God." Other scriptures show that this will be a review of the life we have lived, and the consequences are for eternity. There will be no repetition of life in this world. Those who become children of God through faith in Jesus Christ will spend eternity with Him. Those who reject Him, or neglect His offer of salvation, enter into a place from which the Lord Jesus said there is no escape (Lk 16:19-31). There is no thought of a second chance, or entrance into a new cycle of life. To die in our sins makes permanent the state of being without God and without hope. This gives the greatest possible emphasis to the gospel call, "Behold, now is the accepted time; behold, now is the day of salvation" (2 Co 6:2). Turn to the Lord now, for "if thou shalt confess with thy mouth the Lord Jesus, and shalt believe in thine heart that God hath raised him from the dead, thou shalt be saved" (Ro 10:9).

Where Are the Dead?

158 What assurance do we have that death is not the end of human existence?

The major points of this truth are given us by the Lord Jesus Christ Himself. One statement comes in the narrative in Matthew which describes attempts by certain groups to trap the Lord either in a self-contradiction or in some denial of Scripture. At one point Pharisees, Sadducees, and Herodians followed one another in quick succession. Ordinarily these groups had little to do with each other, but, as with Pilate and Herod who became friends in connection with our Lord's crucifixion (Lk 23:12), these groups joined together in a common cause against Christ.

The Sadducees thought they could demonstrate that the resurrection of the body and existence in a future life are fallacious ideas. They stated a hypothetical case of seven brothers, one of whom married and then died childless. On the basis of the law of levirate marriage (Deu 25:5-6), each of the brothers successively married the woman, each dying without offspring. Finally the woman died. The question was, whose wife should she be in the resurrection, seeing she had been married to all seven?

The Lord did not argue the improbability of the case but revealed that in resurrection, marriage relationships will not be resumed. Heaven is not a projection of earth and its relationships and experiences. We shall be there in a glorified state and on a different basis. The teaching of Scripture did not involve confusion or contradiction. The problem was their lack of knowledge and poverty of faith. Christ said to them, "Ye do err, not knowing the scriptures, nor the power of God" (Mt 22:29).

Various scriptures refer to this subject. The Lord Jesus Christ cited Exodus 3:6, where God revealed Himself to Moses at the burning bush. God referred to Himself as "the God of Abraham, the God of Isaac, and the God of Jacob." The Lord Jesus commented: "For he is not a God of the dead, but of the living: for all live unto him" (Lk 20:38). He gives this as evidence that there will be a resurrection, for if essential life continues after death, and the body is an integral part of man, then we can expect a resurrection of the body, which is what the Bible teaches. Other scriptures show that death is essentially separation of soul and spirit from the body, and they describe the interim state, showing that these parts of man's being continue in conscious existence.

What does the Bible say about the condition of those who have 159 died?

Again it is the Lord Jesus Christ who gives the fullest discussion of this subject. In Luke 16:19-31 He tells of two men who died, one of whom was saved and the other lost. This discourse shows that the experience of death does not necessarily mean entrance into heaven; it can be the gateway to hell. The passage also shows something of the intermediate state between death and resurrection, without going into detail about it. One of these men had lived in luxury, and the other in abject poverty while they were on earth. Now, we read, the beggar was comforted, while the one who had reveled in luxury was in torment. This has often been misinterpreted to mean that all the poor go to heaven and the rich go to hell. What it does show is that earthly success, or the lack of it, is no criterion of eternal state. There will be rich men and poor in heaven; and there will likewise be both in hell. Their being in either place is not related to their financial status while they were on earth.

160 **What does determine the place to which we shall go when we die?**

This is determined by our relationship to the Lord Jesus while we are on earth. Salvation is a present experience, not something we achieve after death. "Behold, now is the accepted time; behold, now is the day of salvation" (2 Co 6:2). The gospel message is always offered for present acceptance, and when we believe, we *are* saved. The possession of eternal life is always stated in the present tense, as in John 3:36: "He that believeth on the Son hath everlasting life: and he that believeth not the Son shall not see life; but the wrath of God abideth on him."

In the day of final judgment the determining factor which condemns those who are there is the fact that they are not found written in the book of life (Rev 20:15). Believers will not be present at that scene: "Verily, verily, I say unto you, He that heareth my word, and believeth him that sent me, hath eternal life, and cometh not into judgment, but hath passed out of death into life" (Jn 5:24, ASV). The King James Version reads, "shall not come into condemnation," but the more accurate text is, "shall not come into judgment." Those who do *not* have eternal life *shall* come into judgment, and the degree of that judgment is determined by the record of their lives—the nature and extent of their deeds.

When a person dies does he go at once to his eternal dwelling 161 place?

No, although the place to which he goes is similar in character. The beggar who died went to "Abraham's bosom," a metaphorical term indicating that he shared the blessedness of Abraham and, by implication, of all those who died in faith (Heb 11:13). This is not actually going to one's reward, as we so often hear, since rewards for faithfulness on the part of believers await the day of Christ. Paul wrote of the "crown of righteousness which the Lord, the righteous judge, shall give me at that day: and not to me only, but unto all them also that love his appearing" (2 Tim 4:8). He did not expect to enter into his reward immediately at death, though he would be "with Christ, which is far better" (Phil 1:23).

Likewise the lost are not immediately judged as to the nature and extent of their misdeeds. This awaits the judgment of the great white throne (Rev 20:11-15). But Luke 16:23 shows that the rich man did immediately enter into torment. It does not appear that the "time" element is part of the judgment, apart from the fact that since death fixes our abode for all eternity, it means that escape from hell is impossible. Some entertain the vain hope that they can exhaust the penalty for sin. The Lord Jesus shows that this is impossible. He quotes Abraham as saying, "They which would pass from hence to you cannot; neither can they pass to us, that would come from thence" (Lk 16:26). But we gather from various scriptures that time is not reckoned in that world. What matters is inexorability. There is no change of condition. It is of the utmost importance that each be saved now—at once.

Shall We Know One Another in Heaven?

The sorrow of parting from loved ones in death is often consoled 162 by the assurance that we shall meet again in heaven. Does the Bible teach that we shall know each other in heaven?

We believe it does, though indirectly, by inference from narrative rather than by direct revelation. When Peter, James, and

John were with the Lord on the mount of transfiguration they saw
and heard Moses and Elijah talking with the Lord Jesus. There
is no indication of an introduction, yet they knew who the two
men were, though of course they had never seen them before.
This suggests that not only shall we know in heaven those we
previously knew on earth, but we shall know everyone there.
Apparently everyone knows everyone. This may be part of the
meaning of 1 Corinthians 13:12, "Then shall I know even as also
I am known."

In the story related by the Lord Jesus in Luke 16, the rich
man in hell retained memory and knew Lazarus. There were
many things he would have liked to have forgotten, but he was
not allowed to. "Son, remember," Abraham said to him. However God will not require believers to remember their sins (Heb
10:17). And since He has blotted them out (Is 44:22), we see
no reason to think we shall remember them. But we shall have
memory, and we shall praise God that Christ has redeemed us
by His blood (Rev 5:9). 1 Thessalonians 4:17 says that at Christ's
coming the dead in Christ shall rise, and we who are alive and
remain "shall be caught up together with them in the clouds, to
meet the Lord in the air: and so shall we ever be with the Lord."
The emphasis here, as elsewhere in the Bible, is on our being
with Christ. Our being caught up *together* refers to the uniting
of living believers with those who had previously died.

163 Does this imply the resumption of earthly relationships?

This would involve serious difficulties. All families are not
united in Christ. Some would be there as complete families, while
others would not. In some families all but one have been saved,
and this would be a cause for constant sorrow. In others husband
and wife are divided, one being saved and the other not. A more
serious difficulty would be a case where husband or wife had
died and the surviving spouse had married again. If earthly
relationships were to be resumed in heaven, this would be a
problem. It was in connection with this point that the Lord
Jesus said, "They that shall be accounted worthy to obtain that
world, and the resurrection from the dead, neither marry, nor

are given in marriage" (Lk 20:35). In this respect they are "equal unto the angels" (v. 36).

Does the Bible explain this change of relationship?   164

Yes. There is an interesting statement in 2 Corinthians 5:16 which is often overlooked. "Henceforth know we no man after the flesh: yea, though we have known Christ after the flesh, yet now henceforth know we him no more." This is a clear and positive statement that we shall not resume earthly relationships in heaven. We believe this explains our Lord's words to Mary at His empty tomb as recorded in John 20:17. The King James Version says, "Touch me not," but authorities agree that a more accurate rendering is: "Do not go on clinging to me." Finding Christ's tomb empty, Mary thought someone had stolen His body. When He revealed Himself to her she evidently fell at His feet and clung to Him, as though to say she would not let Him go again. He then told her the earthly relationship He had had with His disciples as a man on earth would not be resumed. They would have to learn to know Him as their Lord in heaven. The apostle John called himself "the disciple whom Jesus loved." At the last supper he laid his head on Jesus' bosom. Yet when he saw Christ in His ascension glory he fell at His feet as dead (Rev 1:17).

If we do not resume earthly relationships, what is the value of   165 memory?

We believe that while memory will include former relationships, it will be centered in Christ. He is our Saviour, and His love and grace are all-sufficient. In heaven we shall not need the consolation of earthly relationships. These will be remembered as they relate to Christ, and we can mutually rejoice in Him. There is something of a parallel in the contents of the Bible. Many have wondered why whole ancient civilizations are omitted from the Bible. We believe the reason lies in the fact that the Bible tells us of God's dealings and relationships with men. When men turned away from God (Ro 1), He gave them up and called Abram to be the depository of His promises and of the knowledge of Himself. Henceforth the Bible relates only events which have some bearing on His chosen people or His direct dealings with those whose activities had to do with Israel. There is no attempt to record the great civilizations of the earth, much less to preserve the record of them. So in heaven we shall not perpetuate things that were purely human. We shall be occupied there with those things which were related to Him.

166   **Can we offer the consolations of heaven to all who have lost loved ones?**

Very definitely not. Scripture is very emphatic in stating that death fixes our relationship to God permanently. Those who die in faith (Heb 11:13) go at once to be with the Lord. But those who die unsaved are lost forever. The only consolation we can offer an unsaved person facing death is the fact that the door of grace is open so long as he lives. "It is appointed unto men once to die, but after this the judgment" (Heb 9:27). If one dies unsaved there is no consolation in his future, nor can we console those he leaves behind. It is empty words to say one who died in his sins has gone to a better world or that all his sufferings are over. This is the whole point of the warning of the gospel. If we die unsaved, suffering is both intensified and fixed forever.

But for those who have acknowledged their sinful state to the holy God who made us and who have acknowledged as Lord and Saviour His only begotten Son who died for us and rose again, there is redemption and the promise of sharing the glories of our Saviour in the world to come. These hopes are not myth; they are awesome realities. Our thinking has become so humanistic that the idea of accountability to God is either lost sight of or, with many, absolutely rejected. We believe the greatest favor we can bestow on anyone is to make him conscious of his accountability to God and of the way of salvation through the atoning death of Christ and His resurrection. The promise of the gospel is: "Believe on the Lord Jesus Christ and thou shalt be saved, and thy house" (Ac 16:31).

BIBLE INTERPRETATION

Does the Bible Teach Mythology?

Since the Bible speaks of mythological animals like satyrs and 167
unicorns, does this mean that the writers believed in the existence
of these creatures? If so, how does this affect the doctrine of the
divine inspiration of the Bible?

We can say without hesitation that the writers of the Bible
were not guided by mythological beliefs, but that they wrote by
divine revelation and inspiration, and at times with prophetical
insight. However, there are many things about the Bible which
require explanation. No other book in the world has undergone
such careful scrutiny and analysis for so many centuries as the
Bible. The result is that there is a wealth of information about
it available to those who make a study of it. Written in ancient
times, there are many expressions whose meaning would be lost
to us today were there not access to ancient documents and his-
tories. In some cases the meaning of particular words is obscure,
even with the helps available, but there is no vital truth of the
Bible which rests on a precarious foundation. For the most part
the authenticity of the documents is assured, and the meaning of
the text is reliably known. In cases where there is some question
about a particular text or translation, the sense is substantially
known and this does not weaken the divine authority and
reliability of the Holy Scriptures.

What explanation can be given with regard to the creatures 168
named, such as satyrs and unicorns? Are there creatures which
answer to these terms?

The word *satyr* is otherwise translated *hairy one*, or *he-goat*.
However, the same word is rendered *devils* in Leviticus 17:7;

2 Chronicles 11:15. While it could refer to a shaggy animal, it could also be taken in a figurative sense to represent demoniacal appearances. *Unger's Bible Dictionary* states: "Grotesque creatures, half man and half goat, figure in the Greek and Roman mythologies under the name of *satyrs* and *fauns*, but the Old Testament representations are rather demonic conceptions." That is to say, in some passages the word may be taken to represent a goat, while in others it might stand for demonic activity. *The New Bible Dictionary* says: "The precise nature of these 'hairy ones' is obscure. They may have been he-goats in the ordinary sense, or gods having the appearance of goats. Sacrifices were made to them in high places, with special priests performing the ritual." Where this was done among the Hebrews it represented spiritual decline, and the records of it in no wise condone the practice.

The word translated *unicorn* is rather wild ox, and does not refer to the mythical single-horned animal we think of by that name. According to Deuteronomy 14:5 this animal was counted among those permissible for the Israelites to eat, if we accept the identification with the wild ox. Unger thinks the word identifies the ancient auerochs, now extinct, but which were known to exist in Germany in the time of Caesar. It did not probably become extinct in Europe until the Middle Ages, he says. It is not identified with the rhinoceros, nor the modern auerochs, but is believed to have been a powerful animal hunted by ancient kings. This animal had two horns, so the name *unicorn* is a mistranslation.

169   What about other animals which cannot now be identified?

One, mentioned in Job, is *behemoth*. This is taken to mean a great or huge beast, and is usually identified as the hippopotamus. The same word is used elsewhere to signify beasts. There is an obscure reference in Isaiah 13:21 to "doleful creatures," which seems to refer to birds or beasts which emit shrieks or howlings of ominous sound. Unger says the point of reference is that such creatures resort to ruins and deserted dwellings, indicating the desolation which has overtaken them.

The word *leviathan* seems to have had a general rather than specific meaning, and might refer to a crocodile, a serpent, or a sea monster. Isaiah 27:1 may be a reference to the mythological gods of the heathen, whose supposed power would be destroyed by the judgments of Jehovah. The term *dragon* is used in the Old Testament for various creatures, varying from desert animals to the crocodile, whales, or sea monsters. In the New Testament the term *dragon* is found only in Revelation 12, 13, 16, and 20. It is used figuratively, and hence is not to be taken as a description of an actual creature, though it symbolizes a very real being— Satan. Unger says, "In Christian art the dragon is the emblem of sin in general and idolatry in particular, having usually the form of a gigantic winged crocodile." *The Schaff Herzog Encyclopedia of Religious Knowledge* says serpent worship was common in ancient times, and in Assyrian inscriptions one reads of the "great serpent with seven heads." The use of such imagery in the Bible is purely symbolical, and does not indicate belief in their existence as actual creatures.

Can any of the sea monsters mentioned in the Bible be identified? 170

We believe not, with precision. Though the world *whale* occurs in our English Bible, the word in the original text means a sea monster. It could refer to any large fish. In Jonah the term is "great fish," without specifying its identity. While the word in Matthew 12:40 is rendered whale, here also the meaning is uncertain. Deep sea exploration in recent years reveals a far greater variety of marine life than had been known before. There are creatures of varying sizes and shapes, many of them luminous, some attractive to behold, others terrifying. The term *sea-monsters* seems appropriate in describing the denizens of the deep. Had some of these been described in the Bible men would, no doubt, have characterized such descriptions as mythological prior to their discovery.

What can be said about the giants mentioned in Scripture? Are 171 not these relics of ancient mythology?

We believe rather it is the reverse. When the history of these ancient giants is understood, it seems very probable that ancient mythology may be a corrupted account of what really happened.

We know of no history of what happened among men prior to the flood of Noah's time other than the Bible. While there are differences of view among Bible scholars as to the bearing of the opening verses of Genesis 6, we take it to teach that there was an abnormal condition arising from certain commingling of angelic and human beings. The result, according to this passage, was the bringing in of a corrupted race called *nephilim*. While this is translated *giants*, the literal meaning is generally taken to be "fallen ones." However, the general description indicates beings of unusual power, and possibly great stature. There are several other words used for men of great stature and some scholars believe these may have been descendants of these nephilim, though this is questionable, since they would all have been destroyed in the flood. There is the possibility of an occasional liaison after the flood, similar to what took place before. In spite of the obscurity of the record, there unquestionably was, at one time, a segment of the human race who reached giant proportions. Even today there are some who grow to greater physical proportions than the average human being, though these are not related to the race of giants of whom we speak. While these records are not mythological, they may have given rise to the grotesque paraphrases which constitute the mythology of various ancient nations.

Does the Bible Speak About Astrology?

172 Do the heavenly bodies affect life on our planet, and do they carry a message for us?

We believe both things are true within certain limits. The effect of the moon on the tides is well known, and of course life on the earth is dependent on the sun. Stars have been used for navigation and other purposes since ancient times. Psalm 19:1 states that "the heavens declare the glory of God; and the firmament showeth his handiwork." Numerous scriptures speak of this, and Romans 1:20 states that the universal witness of creation to its Creator leaves all men without excuse if they ignore God. The heavens are part of God's creation, and heaven and earth are linked in many ways.

There are two quite different ways of studying the heavens. One is astronomy. It is occupied with the motions and relative locations of celestial bodies, as well as their magnitude, their constitution, etc. This is a mathematical science, and has enabled men to carry out space exploration, including the landing of humans on the moon, and their safe return to earth. The other is astrology; it treats the supposed influence of stars upon human affairs. It purports to foretell terrestrial events by their positions and aspects. But the heavenly bodies do not vary from a fixed pattern which can be ascertained by computers for any given time. This would militate against the idea that human affairs are in any way governed by the coincidental positions of any heavenly bodies. Tides can be predicted accurately long in advance because they are due to fixed relationships. Weather cannot, since it is subject to many variables; and the same is true with human affairs.

Does the Bible speak of astrology, and if so, is it considered a 173 proper field of inquiry for men?

Astrologers are mentioned in the book of Daniel, and once in Isaiah (47:13). Their activities are classified with various occult arts which are condemned in different parts of the Bible. These things were common among people of religions and cultures condemned by the Bible as being contrary to the authoritative revelation of Jehovah, the one living and true God. While the word Chaldean was used for the people who lived in the land of Shinar, in Daniel's day it was applied to a particular group claiming occult powers. Some writers think it referred particularly to astrologers, while that word itself is otherwise translated "enchanters." In any case they are linked together. When Nebuchadnezzar asked his wise men to interpret a dream he had forgotten, they replied: "There is not a man upon the earth that can shew the king's matter: therefore there is no king, lord, nor ruler, that asked such things of any magician, or astrologer, or Chaldean" (Dan 2:10). The category included the entire gamut of magicians and wise men of all sorts.

174 What are some of the ways by which men have endeavored to foretell the future? Does the Bible condone any of them?

There were systems of prognostic magic or divination which included astrology. They were "based on the conviction that any event, good or ill, may be announced or accompanied by some portent observable by men. By knowledge of such portents, men might then foresee impending events or experiences, and welcome or avert them according to their nature. Learned priests systematically compiled long series of omens with interpretations in veritable reference manuals. One such eventually occupied over 170 cuneiform tablets! Omens were either observed from signs in nature or sought by specific techniques." (*New Bible Dictionary*, art. Magic and Sorcery, 2,III,b,ii).

The art of divination is viewed in the Bible as the pagan counterpart of prophecy. Besides the endeavor to foretell terrestrial events by the position of the stars, there were those who claimed to interpret dreams. Others tried to influence the course of events, and so bring things to pass by using charms or casting spells. Such efforts are often associated with demonism. Some persons examined the entrails of animals, particularly the liver, and pretended to read the future by certain markings, much as one might read his fortune in tea leaves, or similar things. Others admitted communication with spirit beings, and some claimed to be in contact with the spirits of persons who had died. This is called necromancy. "Witches" and "wizards" (the male counterpart of witch) claimed supernatural powers, derived either from magical arts or from spirit beings. All of such activity is condemned in Deuteronomy 18:9-12 as having been part of the culture of the heathen people who inhabited the land of Canaan before the conquest by the Hebrews.

175 What, specifically, is wrong with the practice of astrology?

God holds the future in His hands in inscrutability. It can be known by men only as God reveals it. "The secret things belong unto the Lord our God: but those things which are revealed belong unto us and to our children for ever, that we may do all the words of this law" (Deu 29:29). Isaiah speaks of prophecy as being an evidence of the reality and authenticity of the living and true God. "Who hath declared this from ancient time? Who hath told it from that time? Have not I the Lord? and there is no God else beside me; a just God and a Saviour; there is none beside me" (Is 45:21). In the next chapter he writes: "For I am God, and there is none else; I am God, and there is none like me, declaring the end from the beginning, and from ancient times the things that are not yet done, saying, My counsel shall stand, and I will do all my pleasure" (46:9-10). He speaks of this again in chapter 48 with regard to His own people, Israel: "I have declared the former things from the beginning; and they went out of my mouth, and . . . I showed it thee: lest thou shouldest say, Mine idol hath done them; and my graven image, and my molten image, hath commanded them" (vv. 3, 5).

Could astrology and other forms of divination be considered valid   176 as secondary ways of foreseeing the future?

God did not intend man to know the immediate future. "Boast not thyself of tomorrow, for thou knowest not what a day may bring forth" (Pr 27:1). God challenges the devotees of idols: "Produce your cause, saith the Lord; bring forth your strong reasons, saith the King of Jacob. Let them bring forth, and show us what shall happen: let them show the former things, what they be, that we may consider them, and know the latter end of them; or declare us things for to come" (Is 41:21-22). This could include those who try to explain creation itself apart from God. All such activities are viewed as rejection of our dependence upon God for authentic knowledge of the origin of man and the universe. We are equally dependent on Him for knowledge of our eternal destiny. Coupled with this is the fact that we are dependent upon God from day to day, "For we walk by faith, not by sight" (2 Co 5:7). His Word, applied to our lives by the Holy Spirit, gives guidance for daily living. To seek knowledge of the future from other sources implies a deficiency in the provision He has made, and assumes that other sources have authentic value. Neither is true. Other sources are not reliable, and God has given to us "all things that pertain unto life and godliness, through the knowledge of him that hath called us to glory and virtue" (2 Pe 1:3). Let us avail ourselves of the treasures found in the

Bible, and the exceeding great and precious promises it contains, and we shall not need what His Word condemns.

What Is Man's Soul?

177 We read in the Bible of spirit and soul as part of man's being; what are we to understand by these terms?

That there is more to human life than mere physical being and instinct seems evident. People do not respond alike to various conditions. What amuses one person annoys another. What one believes fervently another ridicules. We have certain propensities and characteristics which we call personality. We are "fearfully and wonderfully made" (Ps 139:14), not only physically but also morally and spiritually, and our attitudes and responses can be changed by persuasion or conviction.

Perhaps the subject can be better understood by making certain comparisons. There are various strata in creation. A mineral has form and substance but does not live. Apart from creation itself, it is formed by external forces. It is not born, and it does not die. It does not develop by action of its own and has no consciousness or responsibility. A plant, while composed of mineral matter, has life and is procreated from antecedent life. While some plants, like the giant sequoias, may live for thousands of years, they eventually die. A plant begins life as an embryo and develops to maturity, though it has neither consciousness nor responsibility. A plant normally does not move about, though seeds may become widely scattered by external forces.

An animal, like the plant, consists of mineral matter and also has life and is procreated by antecedent life. It begins as an embryo and develops to maturity. But animals have responsibility, and, except for a few primitive forms, must move about to obtain food for sustenance and in some cases to provide shelter. Unlike plants, animals have consciousness. Trimming a dog's ears would be quite different from trimming a hedge. Animals are largely governed by instinct, though some are capable of strong likes and dislikes. An animal evidently has self-consciousness and many mate with a sense of responsibility for their families. The word "soul" is sometimes applied to animals, and it appears to relate to this element of self-consciousness and responsibility.

How does human life differ from that of the animal?   178

There are those who see only a difference in degree. They consider man to be a kind of exalted animal, going into extinction at death and reverting to the chemical elements of which his body is composed. But the Bible teaches that man is a distinct creation, made in the image of God. By his very nature he is far higher than any animal, for he has a soul that will not cease to live when his body dies. The Lord Jesus said, "Fear not them which kill the body, but are not able to kill the soul" (Mt 10:28). Many other Bible passages speak of man having conscious existence after his body dies. Death for humans is considered to be the departing of soul and spirit from the body (Gen 35:18; Ja 2:26). The apostle Paul speaks of death as departing from the physical sphere in which we live and going to be with Christ (Phil 1:23; 2 Co 5:6-8). Nothing like this is said of any animal. They are "brute beasts, made to be taken and destroyed," we read in 2 Peter 2:12, though we hasten to add this does not suggest cruelty.

Does the soul involve any distinctive feature of man's being?   179

We believe so. In 1 Thessalonians 5:23 the apostle Paul penned a prayer: "The very God of peace sanctify you wholly; and I pray God your whole spirit and soul and body be preserved blameless unto the coming of our Lord Jesus Christ." Many theologians consider that man consists of only two basic parts, the material and the immaterial. Yet even these often distinguish between "animal soul" and "rational soul." In the text quoted, three elements are separated by the conjunction "and," which occurs twice. Only one text mentions spirit in connection with animals, and this does not assert that they have a spirit but raises the question: "Who knoweth the spirit of man that goeth upward, and the spirit of the beast that goeth downward to the earth?"

(Ec 3:21). The question is answered so far as man is concerned
in chapter 12:7: "Then shall the dust return to the earth as it
was: and the spirit shall return unto God who gave it." Man
lives on after the death of the body, and his spirit returns to God
to be dealt with on the basis of his relationship with God prior
to death. There is no suggestion anywhere in the Bible that
animals live on, and the text referred to in 2 Peter indicates that
they do not.

180 What is the distinctive feature of the human spirit?

The Bible nowhere defines the precise nature of the human
soul and spirit, but certain features of them can be discerned
from various references. We have mentioned the lower orders of
creation—the mineral, vegetable and animal—and have been considering the fact that humanity is a distinctive creation of God,
with a far higher responsibility than animals. He not only must
provide for his comfort and sustenance, as the animals, but he
must also prepare for an eternal existence. In one sense, above
man is the angelic creation, beings who are said to be spirit in
their nature (Heb 2:14). Above all is God, the Creator, who is
"Spirit" in the superlative sense (Jn 4:24). With regard to man,
not only are there the material and the immaterial, but there is
also a distinction between the temporal and the eternal. A formula has been suggested which is admittedly oversimplification,
but which may help to clarify our thinking. The body is said to
give consciousness of the world about us; the soul gives self-
consciousness; and the spirit gives God-consciousness. Scripture
is not as definitive as this with regard to these features, and we
are left to draw our own conclusions from what is said about
them.

181 What are some of the references to soul and spirit?

The soul seems to be the basic personality, and man is often
referred to as a soul, but not as a spirit. "Man became a living
soul" (Gen 2:7). "All the souls that came with Jacob into Egypt,
which came out of his loins, besides Jacob's sons' wives, all the
souls were threescore and six" (Gen 46:26). We would get an

entirely different impression if it were said that 66 bodies, or 66 spirits, came with Jacob into Egypt. The soul is spoken of in connection with food (Num 11:6). Such language is not used of man's spirit. On the other hand, "The Spirit itself [Himself] bears witness with our spirit, that we are the children of God" (Ro 8:16). Also, "God is a Spirit: and they that worship him must worship him in spirit and in truth" (Jn 4:24).

The distinction between soul and spirit is not always clear, but we find it difficult to accept the view that they are different aspects of the same part of man's being in view of a passage like Hebrews 4:12: "For the word of God is quick [living], and powerful, and sharper than any twoedged sword, piercing even to the dividing asunder of soul and spirit, and of the joints and marrow, and is a discerner of the thoughts and intents of the heart." Perhaps the tripartite nature of man's being is one of the ways in which he is made like his triune Creator.

What Does the Bible Teach About Hell?

Many people object to the Bible teaching about hell: is this objection justified? 182

There are some who object to the *idea* of retribution for sin. We do not believe such objection is justified, for the whole system of equity in the dealings of God rests on the principle of recompense, whether for good or evil. But for the most part people do not know what the Bible actually says about hell. Perhaps no other doctrine of Scripture is so confused in the minds of people, largely because our English word "hell" is used to translate three different words in the Greek text of the New Testament; and the Old Testament equivalent of one of them is itself translated by three different English words. This promiscuous use of the word "hell" in our King James Version and the lack of uniformity in translating certain other words make it impossible for the ordinary reader to know which word is used in the original text unless he has a Bible which makes this clear by marginal notes. Some versions try to keep the distinctions clear by transliterating certain of these words, but where such distinctions are not made,

readers of the Bible become confused as to what the Bible actually teaches on this subject.

183   What are the words used for "hell" in the Bible?

In the Old Testament the word translated hell is *sheol*, which
is the equivalent of the New Testament *hades*. But *sheol* is not
always rendered hell, but sometimes grave or pit, in spite of the
fact that there are separate words for sepulcher, burying place
and pit. This irregularity in translation has led to the propagation of certain false doctrines regarding the future state. The
New Testament counterpart to *sheol* is *hades*, always translated
"hell," except in 1 Corinthians 15:55 where it is translated "grave":
"O death, where is thy sting? O grave, where is thy victory?"
There is no valid reason for translating "grave" here, and besides,
the more authoritative text is believed to read *thanatos*, "death," in
both clauses of the verse.

But the problem in the New Testament lies in the fact that
our English word "hell" is used about an equal number of times
to translate both *hades* and *gehenna*. A third word is also translated "hell," but this occurs only once, in the verb form, "cast them
down to hell" (2 Pe 2:4). The word here is *tartarus* and refers
to a kind of prison where certain angels were cast who committed a distinctive sin. It does not correspond to either *hades*
or *gehenna*.

184   What is the intended meaning of these words?

The Hebrew word *sheol* corresponds to the Greek *hades* and,
we believe, should not be translated "grave." *Hades* is rather the
region of departed spirits of all mankind. Two derivations are
suggested for the word, one of which signifies "unseen," the
other "all-receiving." In either view the word signifies the spirit
world, unseen by man's physical senses. It is the realm which all
enter at death. By rendering *sheol* as "the grave," it has been
taken to teach that in death spirit and soul cease to have conscious
existence. The translation "the pit" has led some to think the
word signifies a place of torment. Actually *sheol* and *hades* are
used of the intermediate state between death and resurrection,

whether the one who dies is saved or unsaved. Other scriptures show that all exist consciously after the death of the body, saved persons in a state of blessedness in the presence of God and unsaved in a place of judgment.

Sometimes *hades* is used in a metaphorical sense, as when the Lord Jesus warned the people of Capernaum that their city would be brought down to *hades* (Mt 11:23). God deals in judgment upon cities in this world; with individuals the final recompense and compensation come in the next. In this text *hades* is a metaphorical allusion to oblivion. The city as it then existed would cease to be.

What is the meaning of Gehenna?   185

This word signifies what is generally thought of in connection with hell. It is used of the place of torment. The word is a transliteration of the Hebrew *ge-Hinnom*, the valley of Hinnom. It is not known why this valley was named after an obscure person of whom we know nothing except that he had a son. The valley is sometimes called "the valley of the son of Hinnom." It was adjacent to Jerusalem and was the site upon which Solomon built temples to the heathen deities of his wives (1 Ki 11:7-8). These became the scene of human sacrifices in later times (2 Ch 28:3; 33:6), especially in the days of Kings Ahaz and Manasseh of Judah. Such practices were ended when Josiah, the last good king of Judah, made the area a place for the burning of the garbage of Jerusalem (2 Ki 23:10-13). This gave rise to the imagery: "where their worm dieth not, and the fire is not quenched" (Mk 9:44).

However, the Lord uses the term as a prophetic symbol of judgment. The fire is said to be unquenchable (Mk 9:44) and is called "everlasting fire" in Matthew 18:8. He is clearly not speaking of casting unsaved persons into the literal valley of Hinnom but uses the name as a symbol of what is called "the lake of fire" in Revelation 20:10. Death and hell [*hades*] are also said to be cast into the lake of fire (Rev 20:14), death referring to the bodies and *hades* to the souls of those who have died.

186 **If some of these terms are used symbolically, could the fire of hell be symbolic also?**

Hell is described in various ways, though *fire* is one of the most common descriptions. It is called "the blackness of darkness forever" (Jude 13), and the Lord Jesus describes it as a place where "there shall be wailing and gnashing of teeth" (Mt 13:42). Matthew 22:13 also speaks of weeping, and these three passages have been taken to signify remorse, despair and rage. The terms "everlasting," "eternal" and "forever" show that God's judgment is endless. If the fire be symbolic, this would not alleviate the torment involved, as the other figures used show, but it would allow for degrees of intensity in the judgment experienced. Many scriptures show that there will be varying degrees of punishment, just as there will be differing rewards for believers. One such passage is Revelation 20:12, where we are told that unsaved persons are judged on the basis of their deeds while they lived. They are *in* the judgment because their names are not found written in the Lamb's book of life, but the measure of their penalty is on the basis of the record of their lives. The most important issue in the life of every human being is that he make sure he is a child of God in the biblical sense by acknowledging Jesus Christ as Lord and Saviour, by His atoning death and resurrection.

What Is the Unpardonable Sin?

187 **Many persons are deeply concerned that they may have committed the unpardonable sin and so are lost, regardless of their faith in Christ. Is this fear justifiable?**

We believe not. While usually it is the work of a minister of the gospel to persuade people they are lost apart from Christ, many ministers have had to persuade others that they have *not* committed the unpardonable sin. Often a true believer in Christ, one who has trusted Him for salvation, becomes aware of some serious sin in his life. He begins to wonder whether what he has done may be something the Lord can't forgive. The phrase "the unpardonable sin" leaps to his mind and he allows this to trouble him for years. But his very concern about it is evidence that he has not committed this sin.

What is this sin, and where does the Bible speak of it?   188

This sin is referred to in Matthew 12:31-32 and in the parallel passages in Mark 3:28-30 and Luke 12:10. The passage in Matthew reads: "Wherefore I say unto you, All manner of sin and blasphemy shall be forgiven unto men: but the blasphemy against the Holy Ghost shall not be forgiven unto men. And whosoever speaketh a word against the Son of man, it shall be forgiven him: but whosoever speaketh against the Holy Ghost, it shall not be forgiven him, neither in this world, neither in the world to come." Many who are deeply concerned about the pronouncement in verse 32 completely overlook the assurance in verse 31 that every sin and blasphemy except this one can be forgiven. Further, what is condemned is not *sin* against the Holy Spirit, for in a sense, every sin is against Him, but *blasphemy* against Him. This was a specific sin which some whom the Lord was addressing had committed.

What makes this particular sin so serious?   189

It is that it is done deliberately and knowingly. It is not something done in weakness or in ignorance. Such sins are covered by verse 31, and all can be forgiven. The circumstances which led to this pronouncement show what was involved. The Lord Jesus had performed miracles of healing which caused the people to exclaim: "Is not this the Son of David?" that is to say, "Is not this the Messiah?" It seemed a fulfillment of Isaiah 35:5-6 and was so evidently a display of divine power that no other conclusion seemed rational.

All of this was not lost on the Pharisees, who realized that they could not discredit what the Lord had done. Yet they were determined to discredit *Him*. We read in John 12:19: "The Pharisees therefore said among themselves, Perceive ye how ye prevail nothing? behold, the world is gone after him." It was this attitude which motivated them to say, "This fellow doth not cast out devils, but by Beelzebub the prince of the devils" (Mt 12:24). It was a blasphemy against the Holy Spirit, by whose power the miracles were done. It was born of their hatred of Jesus, and they would discredit His works in this way. One committing this sin does not possess a tender conscience and is not troubled about displeasing God. He has rejected God and God's claims upon him.

190 Does this mean that Christ's atonement did not cover this sin, or that it was not sufficient to do so?

No, this is not involved or implied. Since the Lord Jesus Christ was God, manifested in flesh, He was infinite in His being. This gave infinite value to His work. His death was more than sufficient to pay for the salvation of the entire human race. But the atonement of Christ is offered to man on a conditional basis. "Believe on the Lord Jesus Christ, and thou shalt be saved" (Ac 16:31). If and when a person trusts in Him, his sins are forgiven. Peter said, "To him give all the prophets witness that through his name whosoever believeth in him shall receive remission of sins" (Ac 10:43). "The blood of Jesus Christ his Son cleanseth us from all sin" (1 Jn 1:7). There is no thought that the blood of Jesus Christ is less than sufficient to put away every sin. But its effectiveness is conditioned on our faith in Him. None of the sins of an unbeliever are put away, even though the atonement of Christ could do so.

In its very nature the unpardonable sin is an irrevocable rejection of Christ. It bears no relation whatever to sins of the flesh, even where these involve infidelity and seduction, nor to other forms of blasphemy. Serious as these are, they can be forgiven. It was for all the sins of mankind that our infinite Saviour suffered and died. Even an unrepentant attitude is sometimes later broken down and the person becomes saved. Deliberate rejection, including turning others aside by a blasphemous lie against the Holy Spirit, is of such nature that the person is left in his sins. This could not be committed by a believer in Christ.

Does this last part of Matthew 12:32 suggest, as some believe, 191 that some sins can be forgiven after death, in the world to come?

By no means. The text reads: "Whosoever speaketh against the Holy Ghost, it shall not be forgiven him, neither in this world, neither in the world to come." Several different words are used for "world" in the Bible, and the one used here, while often translated "world," also rightly means "age." Read in this way, the text does not refer to another world, but to a future age on this earth. Both in the tribulation time which is prophesied to come on the earth and in the millennium which follows, there will be the forgiveness of sins—but not of this one.

With regard to the possible forgiveness of sins in another world, Scripture is very emphatic: "Now is the accepted time; behold, now is the day of salvation" (2 Co 6:2). Far from holding out any promise of forgiveness after death, Scripture states, "It is appointed unto men once to die, but after this the judgment" (Heb 9:27). Our Lord's revelation of the state of those who have died, in Luke 16:19-31, shows clearly that if a person dies unsaved, there is no possibility of altering his status *then*. The time to be saved is right now, and if you have never done so before, acknowledge Jesus Christ as your Lord and Saviour now.

What Is Meant by "The Ten Lost Tribes of Israel"?

We often hear the expression "the ten lost tribes of Israel." Is this 192 biblical?

This expression, while not strictly biblical, refers to certain events in the history of Israel which are recorded in the Bible. The nation of Israel takes its name from the patriarch Jacob, whose name was changed to Israel after an experience with God which is related in Genesis 32. He had twelve sons whose families became greatly expanded in number during their sojourn in Egypt, and these families became the twelve tribes of Israel, who were formed into a nation under the leadership of Moses at the time of their exodus from Egypt, recorded in the book of Exodus. Later, when the tribe of Levi was separated from the rest to serve in connection with the worship of Jehovah in the tabernacle, in order to have the full complement of twelve tribes, the families of the two sons of Joseph, Manasseh and Ephraim, were each counted as a separate tribe. This was decreed by Jacob before his death (Gen 48:5). In this way Joseph received the double portion which was the right of the firstborn but which Reuben, who was actually firstborn, had lost because of sin (1 Ch 5:1-2).

The nation continued as one until the days of Rehoboam, the son of Solomon, when ten of the twelve tribes rebelled against the leadership of this arrogant young man and established a separate kingdom, known generally as the nation of Israel. The remaining two tribes (Judah and Benjamin) were generally known as Judah, later contracted to "Jews." In their later history these names were used interchangeably, both religiously and politically, but at the time of the division they served to distinguish the two parts of the divided kingdom.

193 How did this division affect the relationship of the nation of Israel to God?

It is interesting to see that God did not entirely give up those who separated, nor did they entirely give up the acknowledgment of God, even though they quickly introduced idolatry. Judah, of course, had the temple and the priesthood; and however unfaithful they were to God, they never officially gave up their allegiance to Him except for a brief time under Ahaz, who imported a heathen altar into the sanctuary compound. Others of the kings of Judah, most notably Manasseh, introduced idolatry, but there was not an official turning away from God as was done in the days of Ahaz.

But in Israel Jeroboam, son of Nebat, their first king, immediately introduced idolatry. He reasoned that if the people were left free to return to Jerusalem to worship, it would lead to the reunion of the nation under the king of Judah. God had promised it would not be so, but Jeroboam did not believe this. Consequently he made two golden calves and set one up in Bethel and the other in Dan (1 Ki 12:28-31). From this idolatry the ten tribes never turned away, though there remained a knowledge of Jehovah, and from time to time God sent prophets to minister to them. So there was a mixed condition of idolatry combined with a profession of faith in Jehovah. No doubt many individuals were truly saved and lived for God, while the bulk of the people apparently did not submit themselves to Jehovah in faith. This was true both in Judah and in Israel.

In what sense did the ten tribes become lost?   194

Each branch of the kingdom, the ten tribes and the two, got so far away from God morally and spiritually that God allowed them to be taken captive by foreign nations. This happened to the ten tribes first, and then, more than a century later, to Judah. The ten tribes were taken into Assyria and never officially returned to their land. The two tribes were taken into Babylon, and in their case there was an official return to Palestine, though many of them did not return.

Some hold to the theory that the ten tribes maintained their national unity and that they have existed as a national entity ever since. This is what is often meant by "the ten lost tribes of Israel." Others hold that, while they did not maintain national unity, certain representative members of them migrated to other lands, and the claim is often made that by the marriage of a prince of one of these tribes to a British queen, the British people have acquired the status of being the Israel of biblical prophecy. We see no basis for this in the Bible and, in fact, believe it is anti-biblical.

Does Scripture give any account of what happened to these   195 tribes?

Only in part. So far as is known, they had no *national* history following their captivity. Before they were taken captive there was a partial reunion with Judah, especially in the days of Hezekiah. In the early days of that monarch he held a great passover to which he invited all Israel. In 2 Chronicles 30:11, 18 we are told that some came from the tribes of Asher, Ephraim, Manasseh, Issachar, and Zebulon. We cannot be sure that these remained in the land of Judah, but it is possible. A few years later the ten tribes were taken captive into Assyria, and this ends their national history so far as the Bible is concerned. There is reason to believe that some from these tribes did later return to their land, and it is believed that in the time of Christ there were representatives of all twelve tribes in the land. Also there were members of all twelve tribes among the "dispersion," as those were denominated who lived outside the land of Palestine.

196 Is there anything in the Bible to discredit the term "the ten lost tribes of Israel"?

Yes, we think so. In the time of Christ those in Palestine maintained a distinction between the bulk of the population and those who were referred to as "Jews." This indicates that many lived there besides the descendants of the two tribes. Further, when Paul defended himself before Festus and Agrippa, in referring to the promise of God to the fathers, he said, "Unto which promise our twelve tribes, instantly serving God day and night, hope to come" (Ac 26:7). Also James addressed his epistle "to the twelve tribes which are scattered abroad" (Ja 1:1). There is no suggestion of any "lost" group. Old Testament prophecies foretell a reunion of all the tribes of Israel (e.g., Eze 37), and the Lord Jesus foretells the gathering of His "elect" from all parts of the earth (Mt 24:31). These include the descendants of Jacob who shall in that day share the faith of their forefathers, but as individuals rather than as an organized group.

Who or What Are Demons?

197 What does the Bible teach about demons?

The word *demon* does not occur in the King James Version of the Bible, though it is found frequently in the original text. One problem with our common version is that often one English word is used to translate several different words in the Greek text. In this case the word *devil* is used for Satan and also the demons. *Devil* (Greek *diábolos*) means "a slanderer." As applied to Satan, it is always in the singular number and is never without the article. In the singular the word is used but once of a person—Judas (Jn 6:70); however, in the plural it is used occasionally to describe people and is translated "slanderers" (1 Ti 3:11), or "false accusers" (2 Ti 3:3; Titus 2:3). In none of these cases does the definite article precede the word.

Demon was a common word in Greek literature and was often used in the sense of a subordinate deity—sometimes in a good sense, perhaps more often in an evil sense. In the New Testament the word always has an evil connotation, and the beings referred to are sometimes addressed by the Lord as "unclean spirits." They are said to be under the leadership of "Beelzebub the prince of the devils" [or demons] (Mt 12:24). The Lord Himself identifies Beelzebub as Satan (v. 26). Hence it appears that the demons are the evil or unclean spirits which constitute the principalities and powers of Satan, the "spiritual wickedness in high places" against which we wage our spiritual warfare (Eph 6:11-18).

Does the Bible tell us the origin of these evil hosts? 198

Not directly, though it seems to imply that they were associated with Satan in his rebellion against God. Even that event is described obscurely. Many Bible students believe two Old Testament passages refer to this event. What is said of the King of Tyrus in Ezekiel 28:11-17 seems hardly applicable to a human, and many believe it refers to Satan in a prehistorical setting. Likewise many believe that Isaiah 14:12-15 looks beyond the king of Babylon and describes the rebellion of Satan. There are substantial grounds for considering that whatever application these passages may have to certain persons, they also give a valid conception of Satan's original rebellion against God. If so, we presume that it was in connection with this event that a large segment of the angels followed him and so constitute an angelic host organized in opposition to God. The expression *principalities and powers* refers to the holy angels in Ephesians 3:10 and to evil angels in Ephesians 6:12. A somewhat obscure passage, Daniel 10:13-21, suggests that these two organized forces sometimes enter into conflict.

199 Does the Bible give any idea of the numbers of these angelic hosts, good or bad?

Not specifically, but there are some suggestions. In one of the visions given to Daniel we read of the throne of God being set ("cast down" in 7:9 should read "placed"), and "thousand thousands ministered unto him, and ten thousand times ten thousand stood before him." These figures indicate that millions of angels are in active service, with hundreds of millions in reserve. Another passage which indicates there are large numbers of angels is Revelation 5:11, where we read of "ten thousand times ten thousand, and thousands of thousands." Even if these figures are not intended to be precise, they suggest enormous hosts of angels.

We are not given any record of the number of fallen angels, but they evidently are also numerous. In Mark 5:9 a demon confessed that his name was "Legion: for we are many." While the Roman legion varied, perhaps between six hundred and six thousand, the word is usually taken to mean a thousand. And since Matthew states there were two men, this would make two thousand demons between them. That this has some validity is suggested by the fact that the demons entered into two thousand swine.

Another obscure reference in Revelation 12:4 states that the dragon with his tail drew the third part of the stars of heaven. The language is obviously symbolic, but some have taken it to mean that Satan controls a third of all the angels. If this be accepted, his hosts are outnumbered two to one, though the decisive factor in all his activities, and those of his hosts, is the omnipotent power of God who made them. If God, for His own purposes, allows the demons to be active in various ways, this does not mean they are beyond His control. A single word spoken in His almighty power would be sufficient to end their activities, at once and forever.

200 What is the activity of the demons?

It appears that their work is the antithesis of that of the holy angels, who are said to be "ministering spirits, sent forth to minister to them who shall be heirs of salvation" (Heb 1:14).

We learn from the different biblical records that demons work to people's disadvantage. In some cases they made men deaf or dumb or subjected them to other serious illness. It is believed they keep some people in a constant state of worry and fear. It is possible that, under the direction of Satan, they are more active than is commonly recognized, since Satan is called "the prince of this world" (Jn 14:30) and "the spirit that now works in the children of disobedience" (Eph 2:2). They may well be the leaders in areas of disobedience to God and in every form of sin and rebellion against all that is good and right and which acknowledges and honors God. They thus lead man to his moral and spiritual destruction.

Can demons attack true believers in Christ, or are they immune to them? 201

There are certain limitations to the power demons can have with regard to the children of God, though Scripture makes it clear that we are not immune to their working. In 1 Timothy 3:7 we read of the possibility of falling into the snare of the devil, and 2 Timothy 2:26 states that this results in our doing Satan's will. Perhaps we see a case of this when the Lord Jesus said to Peter, "Get thee behind me, Satan: thou art an offense unto me: for thou savourest not the things that be of God, but those that be of men" (Mt 16:23). While the word *Satan* means "adversary," it is clear that Peter was at that moment serving the will of Satan.

Yet Satan can never gain possession of us in the sense of ownership, however much he may control us at times. We belong to Christ by right of creation (Col 1:16). But beyond that, the believer belongs to Christ by right of redemption: "What? know ye not that your body is the temple of the Holy Ghost which is in you, which ye have of God, and ye are not your own? For ye are bought with a price: therefore glorify God in your body and in your spirit, which are God's" (1 Co 6:19-20). The power of Satan can never break through this barrier.

PRAYER

Does God Hear the Prayers of Everyone?

202 Can anyone pray? Does God hear the prayers of everyone?

We read in John 9:31 that "God heareth not sinners." But this was not a divine revelation; it was rather the observation of a man who had been blind from birth and who had just received sight by the miraculous power of Christ. As a general statement it may be considered correct, but we should not read theological implications into it. Some have received answers to prayer and have considered this proof they were saved, but this does not necessarily follow.

God stands in a twofold relationship to humanity. He is first of all our Creator and we, His creatures, are dependent on Him. We owe it to God to love and serve Him, and it is right to supplicate His throne about our needs and problems and anything we undertake to do. But sin has come in to separate us from God morally and spiritually (Is 59:2). Each of us is born with a sinful nature (Eph 2:3) which prevents us from enjoying communion with God or properly fulfilling our obligation to Him unless and until we are "born again" (Jn 3:3). In the new birth we receive a new life from God which enables us to serve God.

This brings in our second relationship with God: He is not only our Creator but also our Redeemer, provided we have submitted ourselves to Him in the "obedience of faith" (Ro 16:26). This involves repentance for sin. Acts 17:30 tells us that God "now commandeth all men everywhere to repent." Many persons overlook the fact of sin and erroneously speak of God as the Father of all men, but Scripture says, "Ye are all the children of God through faith in Christ Jesus" (Gal 3:26).

Those who have not become partakers of God's salvation through faith in Christ cannot properly call God their Father in spiritual relationship. Some time ago an actor quoted the Lord's Prayer in the course of his act. Later there was considerable criticism, for many people thought this irreverent. Others thought it was a good thing to do, for, they said, the Lord's Prayer is for everyone. But a Christian writer noted that the prayer begins with the words, "Our Father." This at once confines the availability of the prayer to those who can claim God as their Father in a spiritual sense by the experience of the new birth.

Does this mean that no one should pray to God except those who have experienced personal conversion to Christ? 203

No. All men are still God's creatures, and though their relationship is marred by the presence of sin in their lives, this does not mean that God is unmindful of them. A man has no claims upon God so long as he remains in disobedience and unbelief. Yet there are conditions under which God will hear him.

God is always open to a cry for help or for mercy, and though we cannot guarantee that He will keep us from harm (and this applies to those who are committed believers as well), yet Psalm 72:12 states: "He shall deliver the needy when he crieth, the poor also, and him that hath no helper." Many of us have experienced answers to prayer under these conditions before we ever came into vital contact with Christ by faith. But the promises of God are for those whose lives have been entrusted to Him. Such stand in covenant relationship with God.

Does God give us everything we ask for? What are the limitations? 204

It would require a volume to discuss all that the Bible teaches about prayer, but James 4:3 gives a suggestion: "Ye ask, and receive not, because ye ask amiss, that ye may consume it upon your lusts." The word translated "lusts" does not necessarily have an evil connotation but simply means that the request was made from a selfish viewpoint. In contrast 1 John 5:14-15 says that if we ask anything in keeping with God's will, He hears and answers. There is something similar to this in Psalm 37:4: "Delight thyself also in the Lord: and he shall give thee the desires of thine heart." Delighting ourselves in the Lord implies, not only that what we have asked for is in keeping with God's will, but also that we are in a right spiritual state. Even though we are born again through faith in Christ, there are many things which can mar our fellowship with the Lord. Allowing such things in our lives limits our fruitfulness in prayer, for 1 John 3:20-22 shows that even if our petition is within the scope of God's will, He does not hear us unless we are in a right state of soul.

Several passages of Scripture show that one thing which hinders prayer is an unforgiving spirit. It is in this context that we are told that if we do not forgive others, our Father in heaven will not forgive our trespasses (Mk 11:26). This verse does not say that our entrance into heaven is based on our forgiving others. That would be a precarious ground, for who could be sure that he utterly and frankly forgives everyone who has offended him? Rather it says in the matter of our communion with God, if we are conscious of holding a grievance against another, God will not forgive the things which prevent full communion with Him. This causes our prayers to be ineffective regardless of how fervently we pray.

205 Can we take it as a test that anything we receive in answer to prayer is in God's will for us, while anything we pray for and do not receive is not in His will?

The latter part of this proposition is true if God's withholding is not due to something wrong in our lives. But even then it may have been right to ask. When David, king of Israel, wanted to build a temple for the worship of God, the prophet Nathan at first told him to go ahead with the project. Later he had to return with the message from God that because David was a man of war, God would not permit him to build Him a temple but that David's son would do so. Yet in 2 Chronicles 6:8 we read, "Forasmuch as it was in thine heart to build a house for my name, thou didst well that it was in thine heart." David's state at that point was right, but God saw fit not to allow him to build the temple.

Sometimes God gives us what we ask for even when it is not for our good. One thinks of times when people have been insistent in demanding of God to grant some request. For instance Psalm 106:15 says of the Israelites in the wilderness that God "gave them their request; but sent leanness into their soul." That God granted the request does not prove that it was for their good. God's providences can be considered a general guide but not always a specific one. We are guided more particularly by His Word, which is "forever . . . settled in heaven" (Ps 119:89). If our communion with God is unbroken, we shall have the guidance of the Holy Spirit in understanding His Word.

What Are the Biblical Conditions for Prevailing Prayer?

The Bible says much about God answering prayer. On what conditions will He do so? 206

The privilege of prayer is one of the most potent weapons the Christian has for overcoming adverse forces of any kind. Yet it is often neglected by most believers. Others attempt to avail themselves of this source of power without regard to the biblical requirements for receiving answers to prayer. The result is that they do not receive identifiable answers to prayer. With still others, answers are on such a hit-or-miss basis that they pray without any confidence or expectation of receiving an answer. It is a matter of habit, or at best a pious gesture. But there are many cases where Christians have prayed in faith and God has intervened in a remarkable way. Not only does God intervene in human affairs for the good of His people, but it is evident in Scripture that He intends such intervention to be part of our testimony to Him, to His existence, and to His concern about those who trust in Him. We have such statements as that in Psalm 50:15: "Call upon me in the day of trouble: I will deliver thee, and thou shalt glorify me." Also Isaiah 64:4 reads, in the Berkeley version: "From ancient times men have not heard or perceived, nor has human eye seen a God besides thee who works for him who waits for him." But the Bible gives certain conditions to be met if we are to enjoy this experience.

207 What are some of the biblical requirements for receiving answers to prayer?

Basic to all other requirements is that we be children of God through faith in Jesus Christ. Many persons ignore the claims of God and His proffer of salvation through His Son, Jesus Christ, and yet call upon God when in trouble; and they are annoyed when God does not answer. They have no adequate conception of who God is or of their relationship to Him. Others recite the paternoster, the Lord's prayer, as we commonly call it, overlooking the opening words, "Our Father." Or if they think of them at all, they assume that God is the Father of all mankind. In the Bible we are called God's offspring in the sense that we are His creatures, but the Scriptures also teach that man's spiritual relation to God was broken by sin. Until it is restored by the removal of our sin, we cannot truly call God our Father in the spiritual sense. Scripture states: "Ye are all the children of God *by faith in Christ Jesus*" (Gal 3:26). We are not children of God in the true sense of the word unless we have experienced conversion to Christ and the consequent new birth by the Holy Spirit. Only then can we approach God in prayer as our Father.

208 What are some of the other requirements for receiving answers to prayer?

Another important factor is that it be in the will of God. "This is the confidence that we have in him, that, if we ask anything according to his will, he heareth us: and if we know that he hear us, whatsoever we ask, we know that we have the petitions that we desire of him" (1 Jn 5:14-15). If we ask anything not in God's will we are not likely to receive it. It has been suggested that in eternity we may be as thankful for the requests God didn't grant as for those He did. Sometimes when men are insistent, God gives them what they ask, to their detriment. "And he gave them their request; but sent leanness into their soul" (Ps 106:15).

In Gethsemane the Lord Jesus prayed: "Nevertheless not as I will, but as thou wilt" (Mt 26:39). In my own experience, I always ask God to do according to His wisdom what *He* sees is best and in *His* way.

Are there requirements regarding our state of soul?   209

Very definitely. We read in 1 John 3:20-22: "If our heart condemn us, God is greater than our heart, and knoweth all things. Beloved, if our heart condemn us not, then have we confidence toward God. And whatsoever we ask, we receive of him, because we keep his commandments, and do those things that are pleasing in his sight." It requires a life disciplined by the will of God to put us in a position to expect answers to prayer.

James 1:6-7 emphasizes that our prayer must be of faith: "He that wavereth [doubts] is like a wave of the sea driven with the wind and tossed. For let not that man think that he shall receive anything of the Lord." The element of faith is mentioned in many places in Scripture. The Lord Jesus said, "Whosoever shall say unto this mountain, Be thou removed, and be thou cast into the sea; and shall not doubt in his heart, but shall believe that those things which he saith shall come to pass; he shall have whatsoever he saith. Therefore I say unto you, What things soever ye desire, when ye pray, believe that ye receive them, and ye shall have them" (Mk 11:23-24).

Coupled with faith is persistence in prayer. If our request is not granted, we should continue in prayer until either it is granted or we receive a conviction from the Holy Spirit that it is not in God's will for us. An example of this is when Paul prayed for the removal of the thorn in his flesh and was told by the Lord that it would not be removed. Some men of God have prayed earnestly over long periods before seeing answers to prayer, particularly with regard to the salvation of friends or relatives. We cannot guarantee the conversion of others by prayer, else we should pray for the conversion of the whole world. But if, as we believe, persistent prayer is *one* of the means God uses, we should continue to pray, while also witnessing as God enables.

210 Does not John 14:14 "If ye shall ask anything in my name, I will do it" simplify the whole matter of prayer?

This scripture, like all others, must not be taken in isolation from all else contained in the Bible on the same subject. To interpret the meaning of any passage, we must understand it not only in its immediate context but also within the context of the entire Bible. If our understanding of any passage conflicts with the plain teaching of the Bible elsewhere, we can be sure we are mistaken in our view of the passage under consideration. Scripture does not list all the conditions for receiving answers to prayer upon every reference to that subject. To do so would be cumbersome, and besides, the Bible is purposely so written that it requires searching of its text to learn the truths contained in it. God does not intend to satisfy the curiosity or wishes of the casual reader. If we are not sufficiently concerned about our relationship with God, and our communion with Him, to read and study the Bible constantly, we cannot expect to learn His will accurately. So this statement in John 14:14 must not be taken apart from the various conditions laid down in the rest of Scripture. The thought here seems to be that nothing is too hard for God, and if it is in His will, we can ask in confidence.

What Are "Vain Repetitions" in Prayer?

211 Does our Lord's condemnation of "vain repetitions" mean that we should not pray twice for the same thing?

The question refers to Matthew 6:7, where the Lord Jesus said: "But when ye pray, use not vain repetitions, as the heathen do: for they think that they shall be heard for their much speaking." The primary significance of the verse lies in reference to those religions where certain prayer forms are repeated endlessly with the idea of merit in the act as a religious rite. Christ's teaching was that in prayer we address God, and there is no essential merit in multiplied repetition of words or forms. In some religions prayers are offered by mechanical apparatus, as when they are inscribed on a wooden drum which is then rotated, sometimes by water power; or prayers may be inscribed on pennants which are then placed where they will flutter in the breeze. In other cases a formulary of prayer is created which may be good and right in itself, but then is repeated over and over. Such a practice indicates that the person is not consciously addressing God. To repeat statements endlessly to a friend would be offensive. The Lord Jesus tells us that this also is offensive to God.

Does this militate against other instructions to continue in prayer? 212

No. There are two main categories of instruction regarding constancy in prayer and neither conflicts with Matthew 6:7. One teaches that we should pray to God at all times and in all circumstances. The other instructs us to continue praying until an answer is received. In addition to the general statement: "Ask, and it shall be given you" (Mt 7:7), the New Testament gives many encouragements to pray. Hebrews 4:16 says: "Let us therefore come boldly unto the throne of grace, that we may obtain mercy, and find grace to help in time of need." This is, of course, directed to those who have trusted and acknowledged Jesus Christ as their Lord and Saviour. One delusion many entertain is that they can ignore the claims of Christ, and their need of Him for salvation, and yet turn to God at any time, and have Him at their beck and call to answer their prayers. Such an attitude is a positive insult to God and betrays a total lack of appreciation for who He is, and of our relationship to Him. If we know the Lord and walk with Him we can pray at any time; we are not confined to any special time or place.

Do we have examples in Scripture of the application of these 213 principles?

Two notable examples were given by the Lord Jesus in parables. Each illustrates that it is proper to pray to God at any time of need and that we should persist in prayer until an answer is received. One story is related in Luke 11, where the Lord tells of three friends. One arrived in town late and went to the home of his friend. The host, having no food to set before the wayfarer, went at midnight to a friend of his to ask for bread. The time and circumstances were most inconvenient, yet this man asked, and received, what was needed. Another case is that of a widow who sought justice at the hands of a judge who apparently felt indisposed toward her cause. But her need was urgent, and she would not be turned aside until she received what she required (Lk 18:1-5).

In both instances there was not only the fact of coming at any time of need, but also the thought of persistence in prayer. In the story of the widow the Lord Jesus said: "Men ought always to pray, and not to faint." The word "faint" means to turn coward, or lose heart. A familiar saying has it that "God's delays are not denials." First Thessalonians 5:17 says: "Pray without ceasing." This can be paraphrased, "Don't stop praying." Continue until an answer is given. Daniel prayed for three full weeks about a matter, and when the angel Gabriel was sent to communicate God's answer to him, he was told his prayer had been heard on the first day (Dan 10:12), even though the answer was delayed. He prayed until the answer came.

214 Is it ever right to use the same words in repeated prayers?

Yes, the Lord Jesus Himself did this, we are told in Matthew 26:44. He prayed three times. This is quite different from *reciting* a prayer three times. He prayed to His Father and then returned to His disciples. He went back and repeated the prayer, but it was so far from being a mere recitation that we are told: "His sweat was as it were great drops of blood falling down to the ground" (Lk 22:44). What is condemned is not the restatement of a request, but the repetitive recitation of a form. The apostle Paul prayed three times that his "thorn in the flesh" might be removed (2 Co 12:7-8). We are not to take from these examples that three is the limit for prayer. Each prayed until the answer came. Paul was told that, rather than removing his thorn, God would give him grace to bear it. John 18:11 shows that the Lord Jesus had an answer to His prayer: "The cup which my Father hath given me, shall I not drink it?"

**What are we to learn from this admonition not to use vain repeti- 215
tion in prayer?**

From all the biblical examples cited I would say the obvious
lesson is that we be earnest and direct in our prayers. We should
not simply recite a form of words without special relationship to
the subject of our prayer. It is also implied that prayer should
come from the heart, from our "inner man," and not be just a
mental or verbal exercise. We need to be in communion with
God about the subject of our prayers. This requires that we be
in a right state of soul, so that we are "on praying ground," as
someone has described it. The Bible also gives other conditions
for receiving answers to prayer, an important one being that
the thing requested must be in the will of God. Also, the prayer
must be offered in the expectation of faith, but this is not the
aspect of prayer which is in view in our Lord's remarks in Matthew 6:7. There the thought is rather that the prayer be mean-
ingful and that it be presented as communication with God. It
seems ironical that the pattern of prayer which the Lord gave
in this connection has been used often in a liturgical way, without direct reference to felt needs on the part of the petitioners.
Neglect of the privilege of prayer is a great loss in spiritual
experience.

Should Christians Fast?

**The Bible speaks in numerous instances of fasting: what is in- 216
volved in this?**

The primary idea of fasting is abstinence from food, or at times,
from certain foods. The term is commonly used of religious fasting, though people fast for other reasons also. Different kinds of
fasting are described in Scripture. Luke 4:2 describes our Lord's
fasting in the wilderness: ". . . in those days he did eat nothing."
There was total abstinence from food for forty days and nights.
Daniel 10 speaks of the prophet observing a partial fast. He says,
"I ate no pleasant bread, neither came flesh nor wine in my
mouth, neither did I anoint myself at all, till three whole weeks

were fulfilled" (v. 3). It appears that he restricted himself to a minimum quantity of the simplest foods.

We read that John the Baptist came "neither eating nor drinking." This must be understood in the context of his having been placed under the vow of the Nazarite from his birth (Lk 1:15). This vow required abstinence from wine, strong drink, or anything coming from the vine (Num 6). We learn from Matthew 3:4 that John's food was locusts and wild honey. He did not eat the common food of that day. Other things said about John show that he lived in strict austerity.

217 What is the purpose of fasting?

Many Christians practice some form of fasting or self-denial every day. It is not a matter of ostentation, but it helps to make our body our servant, instead of its being our master. Paul wrote of keeping his body under (1 Co 9:27). David wrote, "I humbled my soul with fasting" (Ps 35:13); and again, in Psalm 69:10, "When I wept, and chastened my soul with fasting."

This frequently accompanied prayer. Esther 4:3 speaks of "fasting, and weeping and wailing"; and chapter 9:31 speaks of "the matter of their fastings and their cry." Daniel says: "I set my face unto the Lord God, to seek by prayer and supplications, with fasting and sackcloth and ashes" (9:3). We are told that King Darius, when he was tricked into putting Daniel into the den of lions, "passed the night fasting" (Dan 6:18).

218 Does the idea of fasting in connection with prayer have divine sanction, or is this only a superstition?

Scripture recognizes this as a proper accompaniment of prayer, and in some cases requires it. In Joel 2:12 we read: "Therefore also now, saith the LORD, turn ye even to me with all your heart, and with fasting, and with weeping, and with mourning." To prevent this being mere outward exercise the next verse says: "And rend your heart, and not your garments, and turn unto the LORD your God; for he is gracious and merciful, slow to anger, and of great kindness, and repenteth him of the evil." The disciples of Christ on one occasion asked Him why they could not cast out a certain demon. He replied: "This kind can come forth by nothing but by prayer and fasting" (Mk 9:29). Fasting has its place in the economy of God.

Is this to be done at certain appointed seasons? If not, when is it appropriate to fast? 219

In the Old Testament certain times of fasting were prescribed by the law, as in Leviticus 16:29. The expression, "afflict your souls," implies fasting. But fasts were also proclaimed on special occasions, whenever there was a special need to draw near to God. In Ezra's time, when they were returning to Jerusalem from Babylon, and reached a critical point in their journey, Ezra proclaimed a fast "that we might afflict ourselves before our God, to seek of him a right way for us, and for our little ones, and for all our substance" (Ezra 8:21).

The Lord Jesus fasted before meeting the temptations of Satan. Our Lord's remark about John the Baptist (Mt 11:18) implies that John made it a habit of life to fast. This was true also of the apostle Paul, who spoke of being "in fastings often" (2 Co 11:27). Some of these may have been involuntary, due to his circumstances, but he speaks of it in chapter 6:5 as though it were a habit of life. In 1 Corinthians 7:5 he implies that this would be desirable for others to follow, although the expression "and fasting" is not in some manuscripts. We read also of Anna the prophetess, at the time of Christ's birth, serving God with "fastings and prayers night and day" (Lk 2:37). Acts 13:2 speaks of the prophets and teachers at Antioch fasting, along with prayer, and these are mentioned also in Acts 14:23. Likewise Cornelius, the Roman centurion, was fasting when God sent an angel to communicate with him (Ac 10:30).

Are there other forms of fasting besides abstinence from food? 220

Yes. In fact the prophet Isaiah saw in the fasting of Israel much the same ostentation, without inward reality, that the Lord Jesus saw in the Pharisees of His day. One of the latter boasted, "I fast twice in the week" (Lk 18:12). Probably the custom was to fast one day a week. The Pharisee doubled up on that, and wanted everyone to know it. The Lord condemned this kind of thing (Mt 6:16-18). He does not condemn fasting, but instructs that it should be done before God, and not to receive accreditation from men because of it.

Isaiah, writing seven centuries before Christ, speaks to the same situation.

> "Wherefore have we fasted, say they, and thou seest not? wherefore have we afflicted our soul, and thou takest no knowledge? Behold, in the day of your fast ye find pleasure, and exact all your labours. Behold, ye fast for strife and debate, and to smite with the fist of wickedness: ye shall not fast as ye do this day, to make your voice to be heard on high. Is it such a fast that I have chosen? a day for a man to afflict his soul? is it to bow down his head as a bulrush, and to spread sackcloth and ashes under him? wilt thou call this a fast, and an acceptable day to the LORD? Is not this the fast that I have chosen? to loose the bands of wickedness, to undo the heavy burdens, and to let the oppressed go free, and that ye break every yoke? Is it not to deal thy bread to the hungry, and that thou bring the poor that are cast out to thy house? when thou seest the naked, that thou cover him; and that thou hide not thyself from thine own flesh? Then shall thy light break forth as the morning, and thine health shall spring forth speedily: and thy righteousness shall go before thee; the glory of the LORD shall be thy rereward" (Is 58:3-8).

Interestingly, Isaiah then goes on to speak of receiving answers to prayer, showing that it is not physical fasting alone that establishes this kind of communion with the Lord, but far more, the spiritual fasting of which the physical is a symbol, though the latter does help to keep our bodies under (1 Co 9:27).

THE HOLY SPIRIT AND GIFTS

What Is the Baptism of the Holy Spirit?

**Many people speak of the baptism of the Holy Spirit as a second   221
work of grace; is this a biblical term?**

The term is not used in the Bible, but the Bible does speak of
the glorification of the believer at the coming of Christ for His
own as "the glory that shall be revealed." This might be termed
"a second work of grace," but it has no reference to the baptism
of the Holy Spirit. The first work of grace was salvation: "For by
grace are ye saved through faith; and that not of yourselves: it is
the gift of God: not of works, lest any man should boast" (Eph
2:8-9). The believer's entire life is a record of "grace upon
grace," but 1 Peter 1:13 speaks of our coming glory as "the grace
that is to be brought unto you."

Our salvation is an accomplished fact as soon as we submit
ourselves to Christ in the obedience of faith, acknowledging Him
as our Lord and Saviour. Our sins are forgiven (Ac 10:43) and
we are made children of God by new birth (Jn 1:12-13). We do
not need any second work of grace for this. But we are told in
Romans 8:22-25 that though we now have the firstfruits of the
Spirit, we are yet waiting for the redemption of our bodies. It is
the application of redemption to our bodies which will constitute
God's second work of grace.

**How does the Bible describe or define the baptism of the Holy   222
Spirit, and when does it take place?**

In Acts 1:5 the Lord Jesus told His disciples that they would
be baptized with (or, in) the Holy Spirit "not many days hence."
It seems clear that this baptism of the Holy Spirit took place on

the day of Pentecost. Though the word "baptism" is not used in describing the event, the apostle Peter definitely associated "baptism" with this event when, in Acts 11:15-17, he described to the church at Jerusalem what took place in the household of Cornelius, the Roman centurion. That experience was similar to what had happened to the believers at the beginning, i.e., on the day of Pentecost, and it reminded him of a previous statement of the Lord: "John indeed baptized you with water; but ye shall be baptized with the Holy Ghost." This identifies the experience in this terminology.

The only place where the spiritual result of this baptism is discussed is 1 Corinthians 12:13, where we read: "For by one Spirit are we all baptized into one body, whether we be Jews or Gentiles, whether we be bond or free; and have been all made to drink into one Spirit." No other explanation of the baptism of the Spirit is given.

223 In both Acts 2 and Acts 10 a feature of this experience was the accompanying gift of tongues. Are we to assume that this gift always accompanies the baptism of the Spirit?

No, and it is a striking fact that in only three passages is speaking in tongues mentioned in connection with the baptism of the Holy Spirit, though it may be implied in a fourth case. These are at the first giving of the Spirit (Ac 2), in the household of Cornelius (Ac 10), and with the converts who had been disciples of John the Baptist (Ac 19). The case where it seems to be implied is the conversion of the Samaritans (Ac 8). In each of these there was a special need for authentication, in view of the change of dispensation involved and the resulting unity of believers from whatever origin.

In Acts 2, these special demonstrations took place on the birthday of the Church, marking the beginning of the new dispensation. Acts 8 gives us the conversion of the Samaritans with whom, previously, Jews had no dealings. This momentous occasion required a special demonstration of divine power to make the Samaritan Christians acceptable to the Jewish believers. Acts 10 relates the conversion of Gentiles, and we see from chapter 11 that had there been no such demonstration of divine power, the

Gentiles would not have been received on equal grounds with those already saved, if they would have been received at all. The remaining case, in Acts 19, dealt with some who had been converts of John the Baptist. It is highly significant that there is no other mention of speaking in tongues in the book of Acts; and in the rest of the New Testament the subject is discussed but once—in 1 Corinthians 12-14. In all other references the word "tongue" means either the member of the body or a language. In no other case is speaking in tongues connected with salvation or with the baptism of the Holy Spirit.

If a person does not speak in tongues, how can he know he has 224
experienced the baptism of the Holy Spirit?

By the Word of God, which tells us that by one Spirit we are all baptized into the body of Christ (1 Co 12:13). Some hold that the baptism of the Spirit in Acts 2 is the only baptism, and that we each share in that as we become saved; but the fact that those in the household of Cornelius experienced the same thing convinces me that each of us is baptized into the body of Christ at his conversion. We do not need any authenticating sign, and the great bulk of believers throughout this dispensation have never spoken in tongues. Yet they have demonstrated the fruits and power of the Holy Spirit in their lives. We believe it is a basic principle with God that we have far more assurance through resting on the statements of His Word than through trusting in experience alone.

Is the baptism of the Spirit to be equated with salvation? 225

No, but it accompanies salvation in this dispensation. That the Lord Jesus speaks in Acts 1 of the baptism of the Spirit as being yet future does not suggest that people were not saved up until then. In fact the very persons who experienced that baptism in Acts 2 had been believers in Christ and already knew the forgiveness of sins and had been born again in the biblical sense of that term. The Holy Spirit was given in a special way in this dispensation, uniting believers of all previous backgrounds into one body in Christ and indwelling every believer as a personal presence. From the time of His advent all believers have been united in the spiritual body of Christ, and each is indwelt by Him. These are distinctive features of this Church Age.

What Place Does the Holy Spirit Have in Creation and Redemption?

226 If the Holy Spirit is part of the Deity, does this mean He participates in such acts of God as creation and redemption? If so, what part does He have?

Scripture teaches that the Holy Spirit participated directly in both creation and redemption, as He does also in all the works of God. Certain acts of creation are specifically ascribed to the Holy Spirit. Psalm 104:29-30 not only ascribes creation to Him, but the passage is taken by some to suggest the possibility of successive creative acts in the past, which might account for the appearance of varying forms of life at different times. The passage says, "Thou hidest thy face, they are troubled: thou takest away their breath, they die, and return to their dust. Thou sendest forth thy spirit, they are created: and thou renewest the face of the earth." With regard to the original creation of the universe we read in Job 26:13: "By his Spirit he hath garnished the heavens"; and Genesis 1:2 shows His continuing care over that creation when it was in a chaotic state: "The Spirit of God moved [or, brooded] upon the face of the waters."

Job 33:4 attributes our own creation to the Holy Spirit: "The Spirit of God hath made me, and the breath of the Almighty hath given me life." It has also been thought that Psalm 8:3—"When I consider thy heavens, the work of thy fingers, the moon and the stars, which thou hast ordained"—contains a reference to the Holy Spirit. "Thy fingers" is taken to be a reference to the working of the Holy Spirit. In Matthew 12:20 the Lord Jesus spoke of His casting out demons by the Spirit of God, while a similar passage in Luke says, "If I with the finger of God cast out devils . . ." (Lk 11:20). The reference to fingers suggests precise placement or applied power and ultimate effect. This does not eliminate the part of the Father and the Son in creation, but it warrants the inclusion of the Holy Spirit in this work. All of this indicates the unity and equality of the three Persons of the Holy Trinity.

Is this true with regard to the work of redemption also? 227

Yes, both with regard to Christ's accomplishment of the work necessary for redemption and also with regard to our participation in it. In connection with the death of Christ, we are told in Hebrews 9:13-14 that it was through the eternal Spirit that He offered Himself: "For if the blood of bulls and of goats, and the ashes of an heifer sprinkling the unclean, sanctifieth to the purifying of the flesh: how much more shall the blood of Christ, who through the eternal Spirit offered himself without spot to God, purge your conscience from dead works to serve the living God?" This illustrates how the three Persons of the Holy Trinity are involved in any work: Father, Son, and Holy Spirit each have part in it.

How does this apply to the individual's reception of the benefits 228 of Christ's atonement?

The Holy Spirit has a large part in the individual's participation in the benefits of Christ's redemptive work. It is He who works conviction in our hearts. "When he is come he will reprove [or, convict] the world of sin, and of righteousness, and of judgment" (Jn 16:8). He sanctifies or sets apart to God those who respond to His working in them (1 Pe 1:2). Also it is by His power that we are regenerated, for we read in John 3:5 that "except a man be born of water and of the Spirit, he cannot enter into the kingdom of God." We take the water to be typical of the Word of God, since this identification is made in Ephesians 5:26; and the Word of God is said to be the instrument by which we are born again (1 Pe 1:23; Ja 1:18). But John 3:6 shows that the source of eternal life is the Holy Spirit: "That which is born of the flesh is flesh; and that which is born of the Spirit is spirit." So the Holy Spirit not only participated in Christ's offering of Himself to God, but He also has an active part in making His redemption effective in the life of the believer.

229 **If the works of Christ were performed in the power of the Holy Spirit, what does this suggest with regard to the believer's service for Christ?**

It implies, of course, that our service for Christ must also be by the power and leading of the Holy Spirit; and this is clearly stated in various texts of Scripture. This is especially true with regard to certain official work, such as the writing of the Holy Scriptures. Numerous passages speak of His guiding and controlling the writers of the various parts of Scripture, so that the end result was an authoritatively communicated Word of God.

But it is not only official works which require the leading and energizing of the Holy Spirit. In the New Testament record we find Him leading men in their fields of service. Acts 16:6-10 gives an illustration of such guidance. Here the Holy Spirit forbade one area of service to the apostle Paul and his party while opening another to them. Earlier, in chapter 13, the Spirit designated Barnabas and Saul (or Paul) for missionary work, and it was He who sent them forth. We see also in the Old Testament a wide range of activity of the Holy Spirit in the lives of various servants of God. This is widened in the New Testament to include every believer, since each is indwelt by the Holy Spirit.

230 **Is there any specific statement of the place the Holy Spirit has in ordering the lives of believers in this dispensation?**

In 1 Corinthians 12:4-6 we have an interesting reference to the working of each of the Persons of the Holy Trinity with regard to the conduct of the work of the Lord: "Now there are diversities of gifts, but the same Spirit. And there are differences of administrations [or, services], but the same Lord. And there are diversities of operations, but it is the same God which worketh all in all." In this passage we see the varying functions of the Father, the Son, and the Holy Spirit, harmonizing to accomplish the purposes of God through His servants. But not only does the Holy Spirit impart spiritual gifts; He also enables us to use the gifts effectively. Far from ignoring the Holy Spirit, the Scriptures teach that the Christian life can only be a fruitful, satisfying experience when we live in His grace and power.

Is the Gift of Tongues for Us Today?

We hear a great deal about the gift of tongues: does the Bible 231 teach that this gift is for us today?

I do not believe so. The gift of tongues was one of a number of things mentioned as signs given to authenticate the gospel message. This was especially necessary since the truths which led to the establishment of the Church vitiated the Levitical system of approach to God which had been established in the days of Moses. Since that system was given by divine revelation, the Jews clung to it and did not accept the fact that it was a temporary arrangement and that God could give a further revelation which would not require either a temple or its priesthood and sacrifices.

The law and its ritual had stood for 1,500 years and thus seemed quite permanent, but the apostle Peter tells us that in some respects a thousand years is with the Lord but as a day. Their own Scriptures taught a similar truth, for Moses said, in Psalm 90:4, "A thousand years in thy sight are but as yesterday when it is past, and as a watch in the night." The law itself had been authenticated by divine signs. Moses did not simply announce to Israel that they were under law. God set apart Mount Sinai, and a law was given that any man or beast touching the mountain would be put to death. God caused the mountain to quake and smoke, and there was the sound of a trumpet rising to a crescendo, so that the people were afraid and asked Moses to speak to God on their behalf. Even Moses said, "I exceedingly fear and quake" (Heb 12:21). So when Moses came down from the mountain with the tables of the law there was no question of their divine origin, or of that of the other laws and regulations which he promulgated at that time. However the mountain did not continue to quake and smoke. It was a temporary sign for the authentication of the law; and so, we believe, with the gift of tongues and similar sign gifts. They served the temporary purpose of validating the gospel message and the establishment of the church.

232   What identifies tongues as a sign?

The Lord Jesus called tongues a sign, along with certain other
miraculous gifts, in Mark 16:17-18. He said, concerning the
preaching of the gospel, "These signs shall follow [accompany]
them that believe; in my name shall they cast out devils; they
shall speak with new tongues; they shall take up serpents; and if
they drink any deadly thing, it shall not hurt them; they shall
lay hands on the sick and they shall recover." Some authorities
leave out the word "new" before tongues, and many scholars feel
that the entire last 12 verses should be omitted, though the mass
of manuscripts contains them.

The Lord promised that these signs would accompany believers, and verse 20 states that this was the case. Hebrews 2:3-4
confirms this: "How shall we escape, if we neglect so great salvation; which at the first began to be spoken by the Lord, and was
confirmed unto us by them that heard him; God also bearing
them witness, both with signs and wonders, and with divers
miracles, and gifts of the Holy Ghost, according to his own will?"
In Mark 16 tongues are included with other miraculous sign gifts,
and both Mark 16 and Hebrews 2 show that they were given to
validate the gospel message, especially its going out to all nations.

233   What was the gift of tongues?

The initial giving of the gift of tongues shows the nature of
the gift. On the day of the Jews' feast of Pentecost the disciples
were sitting in a house, and there was a sound like a rushing
mighty wind, and cloven tongues of fire sat upon each of them.
At the same time they were filled with the Holy Spirit and began
to speak with other tongues, which is to say, in languages other
than those with which they were familiar. Since Pentecost was
one of the occasions when all the males of Israel were required
to appear in Jerusalem (Deu 16:16-17), people were present
from some fifteen or more foreign countries. They all heard the
disciples speak in their own languages.

From this we gather that the gift of tongues was a divine
enablement to speak in a foreign language one had not studied
or known. First Corinthians 14 speaks of "unknown" tongues,

but it should be noted that the word "unknown" does not occur in the original text. It is simply "a tongue," or language. Some have thought that 1 Corinthians 14:14 implies ecstatic utterances, not constituting any known language, but we do not believe this is justified here or in any other New Testament reference. Revelation 5:9 speaks of some being redeemed "out of every kindred, and tongue, and people, and nation." "Tongue" seems to signify every language common to man and has no reference to ecstatic utterances.

How was this gift given, and should we seek it today?   234

At its inception is was given by an act of God, and there is no record of anyone receiving it by seeking. In fact 1 Corinthians 14:12 seems to teach that we should seek other gifts rather than this one. It is interesting that speaking in tongues is mentioned, other than the day of Pentecost, only in Acts 10:46 and 19:6, though it may be implied in the happening in Samaria in Acts 8. Each of these was a special case, having to do with the transition from Judaism to the Church position. We know of no reason to think that the gift should be sought if it is not freely given from God.

Why and when was the gift withdrawn?   235

It is often assumed that failure to speak in tongues is due to lack of faith or devotion to God, but we do not believe this is the case. Rather we believe the gift was withdrawn because it had served its purpose. Many think that 1 Corinthians 13:8-10 teaches that when the Bible should be completed the gift of tongues would cease. While historically this was about the time of the cessation of the gift, we do not take this to be the meaning of that text. Nor was it withdrawn at one stroke, comparable to the giving of the gift. Instead it appears that those having the gift continued to exercise it. In fact 1 Corinthians 12-14 indicates an abuse of the gift. But we believe that God ceased giving the gift because it was intended as an authenticating sign and not a permanent feature of this dispensation. It is never said to be a proof of salvation or of the indwelling presence of the Holy Spirit.

Does the Bible Teach Divine Healing?

236 **We read in the Bible of gifts of healing: does this mean that we should not use medicines?**

Miraculous healing was not universal even when the Lord Jesus was on earth. It was a specific grace from God to heal certain persons. It was never proclaimed as a right, either for humanity generally or for all believers. Christ's miraculous healing was one of the evidences to confirm His claim that He had been sent from God; and He gave the power of healing to some of His disciples to confirm that the gospel they preached, and the new revelation which accompanied it, were from God. The exercise of this power constituted a special sign.

Sickness is part of the law of death which works in our bodies as the result of sin. We do not mean a person's own sin, though that can be a contributing factor, but we mean that the entrance of sin into human experience brought the sentence of death. In the wisdom of God He did not make physical death immediate, but a law of death began to work in man, eventuating in the experience of death itself. At the same time, God was pleased to put into the human body tremendous powers of recuperation and healing, so that often very serious diseases are healed and overcome by what we call "natural processes." In that sense, all healing is from God, but this does not eliminate the use of medicines; it rather encourages their use.

237 **Does the Bible speak of the use of medicines and the services of doctors?**

Yes, it speaks of both. Luke, who was Paul's companion and who wrote the gospel which bears his name as well as the book of Acts, is called "the beloved physician" (Col 4:14). This suggests that his services were welcomed. Also, the Lord Jesus said on one occasion, "They that be whole need not a physician, but they that are sick" (Mt 9:12). This implies that the normal procedure when someone is sick is to call a physician.

As to the use of medication, Jeremiah 8:22 has been made familiar by the often-sung spiritual: "Is there no balm in Gilead;

is there no physician there? why then is not the health of the daughter of my people recovered?" Jeremiah 46:11 says, "Go up into Gilead, and take balm, O virgin, the daughter of Egypt: in vain shalt thou use many medicines; for thou shalt not be cured." These references imply that normally medicine aids the healing and curing processes; but there was no cure for the sickness here described, because it was of a spiritual nature. Proverbs 17:22 says, "A merry heart doeth good like a medicine." Ezekiel 47:12 describes a millennial scene in which the leaves of trees will yield medicine. This is referred to also in Revelation 22:2. There are various references also to ointments, and though these were sometimes used for the scent, some were also used to aid the healing process, as in Isaiah 1:6. In Revelation 3:18 the Lord Jesus refers to the use of eyesalve. While this is a metaphorical usage, it has its basis in the normal use of such ointment.

Does not "faith healing" honor God more than the use of medicine and the services of doctors? 238

Faith means believing and acting on God's Word. If we do not have a command or promise from God as the basis of our belief and action, it is not the exercise of faith. Faith does not mean that we determine an objective and then assume that God will fulfill it if we proclaim our dependence on Him to do so. Many have adopted that idea, but it is rather related to the pagan idea that abstract faith has force. Faith is not an abstract principle; it is confidence in God, shown by believing and accepting His revelation of Himself and acting upon the call or instruction of His Word. Consequently we do not honor God by deciding that He must heal us apart from the means He makes available to us. It would be like a farmer saying that since he trusts God for his crops he will neither sow nor reap. To act in this way would be folly. Or it would be like a housewife refusing to stock her pantry with food and making no effort to prepare a meal, but depending on the Lord to feed her family. It is God who gives us the power to plant and harvest and who makes the fields fruitful, but He requires that we do what He enables us to do and gives us intelligence for. So it is with the healing of bodily ailments. We honor God only when we act on His Word, not according to standards of our own devising.

239 Does not Christianity teach that Christ's atonement includes the healing of the body?

If it did, there would be no reason why a Christian should die, if he continues in faith, unless there is a time limit to this power. But we do not believe that Christ's atonement includes bodily healing. In fact, it seems to be expressly denied in Romans 8:19-25. Beginning at verse 22 the passage reads: "For we know that the whole creation groaneth and travaileth in pain together until now. And not only they, but ourselves also, which have the first-fruits of the Spirit, even we ourselves groan within ourselves, waiting for the adoption, to wit, the redemption of our body. For we are saved by hope: but hope that is seen is not hope: for what a man seeth, why doth he yet hope for [it]? But if we hope for that we see not, then do we with patience wait for it." This clearly states that although we have the "firstfruits of the Spirit," our bodies are not yet redeemed. The redemption price was paid on the cross, but when it is applied to our bodies the result will be not healing, but glorification (v. 30). Meantime we share the groaning of creation and the physical distresses which are implied in this. Our souls are saved (1 Pe 1:9), and our bodies will be glorified at Christ's coming to take us to be forever with Himself (1 Th 4:13-18).

240 Does God ever heal miraculously, and if so, on what basis?

Quite clearly God has, on numerous occasions, either healed people miraculously and instantaneously or has caused healing to come about when by any normal prognosis the person would be doomed to an early death, or to a lifetime of suffering and deformity. We have records of this in the Bible, and there have been numerous cases of this kind in the history of the church. As to why it is done at times and not universally or commonly, the basic reason lies in God's own will with regard to the matter. God performs miracles when it serves some purpose of His own. It is not always a matter of the person's need, nor of the fervency of faith, either on the part of the sick one, or of those who pray for him. A study of the context of James 5:15 will show that this is no exception, though verses 15 and 16 show clearly that it is proper to pray for the healing of a sick person. If someone is afflicted, he should pray. If he is merry, he should express his joy in praise to God (v. 13). If he is sick he should cast himself upon the mercy of the Lord. Many expositors think that anointing with oil was a common treatment of that time and that it did not have any special spiritual significance. The balance of the verse implies a dealing with God on the part of both the sick person and the elders. That the statement "The prayer of faith shall save the sick" was not an absolute is shown by experience. Had it been so, Christians need never die. It would be outrageous to suggest that all who have died did so because their faith failed. It is a general principle that God answers prayer according to His own will.

How Can We Recognize a Person Who Is Filled with the Holy Spirit?

Does being filled with the Spirit involve our doing miraculous 241 feats?

Not necessarily. One gathers that the Bible speaks of the power of the Holy Spirit in the life of a believer in more than one aspect. With regard to the indwelling presence of the Holy Spirit, our being filled has to do with the development of Christian character. With regard to His coming upon us, our being filled with the Spirit has to do with the performance of some act or service for Him. The one has to do with our mode of living and our inward attitudes and reactions. The other has to do with our activities. Sometimes the Spirit of God comes on a person in power without that person even being saved. An Old Testament example of this is Balaam, and one in the New Testament is Judas. In such cases there is no credit to the person for anything he does, even though it be prophesying, as with Balaam, or casting out demons and other acts of power, as with Judas. The deeper and more important aspect of the power of the Spirit of God in us is seen in our daily life and character.

242 Where does the Bible describe this aspect of the fullness of the Holy Spirit?

Perhaps the most complete statement is found in Galatians 5:22-23, where we have a ninefold description of the *fruit* of the Spirit. This fruit is a resultant state, or character, produced by one's being filled with the Spirit. The passage says, "The fruit of the Spirit is love, joy, peace, longsuffering, gentleness, goodness, faith, meekness, temperance [self-control]." These are not the product of effort, but they develop as we "walk in the Spirit" (i.e., as our lives are controlled by Him). These nine things fall into a natural division of three triads, the first having to do chiefly with our communion with God; the second, with our relations with others; and the third, with our inward state—self-discipline. They are not cultivated separately, but all nine develop together. It is the fruit of a life lived in submission to God.

Sometimes the fullness of the Holy Spirit is accompanied by an experience of suffering, and seeming defeat, instead of the opportunity to accomplish great exploits. The three young Hebrews "quenched the violence of fire" (Heb 11:34), but the martyrs who were burned at the stake were no less filled with the Spirit. And while some, by faith, "turned to flight the armies of the aliens," no less filled with the Spirit were those who "wandered about in sheepskins and goatskins; being destitute, afflicted, tormented; (of whom the world was not worthy)" (vv. 37-38).

243 Where in the Bible do we read of the Spirit coming on a person in power?

In Numbers 23 and 24 are recorded four prophecies given by Balaam, every one of which was evidently a message from God. His reference to the "Star of Jacob, and a Scepter . . . out of Israel" (24:17) is thought by many to have been the basis for the visit of the Magi when Christ was born. In connection with the third of his messages, we are told: "Balaam lifted up his eyes, and he saw Israel abiding in his tents according to their tribes; and the spirit of God came upon him. And he took up his parable and said . . ." (24:2-3). And Balaam introduced his last message: "He hath said, which heard the words of God, and knew the knowledge of the most High, which saw the vision of the Almighty, falling into a trance, but having his eyes open: . . ." (v. 16). Yet we learn from several references to Balaam in the New Testament that he was not a saved man, though the Holy Spirit furnished him with divine power for this occasion. Another Old Testament example is Samson. Though he lived in sin much of the time, we read of one occasion: "When he came to Lehi, the Philistines shouted against him: and the Spirit of the Lord came mightily upon him, and the cords [ropes] that were upon his arms became as flax that was burnt with fire, and his bands loosed from off his hands" (Judg 15:14). God can impart power to any creature to accomplish His purpose at a given time. The same was true of Judas, who was one of the group of twelve disciples to whom the Lord gave power to "heal the sick, cleanse the lepers, raise the dead, cast out devils [demons]" (Mt 10:8). We know of no reason to think that Judas did not exercise this power, yet in John 6:70 the Lord Jesus said of him: "Have not I chosen you twelve, and one of you is a devil?"

How are these two types of the Holy Spirit's control related ?   244

In the one case it consists in His laying hold of a person by His divine power, regardless of that one's spiritual condition. For this, one need not even be saved, as with Balaam or Judas, or be spiritually motivated, as with Samson. In the other case the filling of the Holy Spirit is dependent not only on the person's being born again through faith in Christ but on his yielding his life to the control of the Holy Spirit. It is not a mysterious experience but a day by day mode of living. It requires constant feeding of our souls on the Word of God and communion with God in prayer. It means also that we live in the awareness of opportunities to serve the Lord by serving others and taking advantage of opportunities to share our faith with those around us. Spectacular demonstrations of power do not necessarily authenticate the one who performs them. Such a demonstration could be an example of God's fulfilling His will in spite of the person. Also, sometimes the power is from an evil source, as will be the case with Antichrist. So while we need divine power to accomplish God's purposes in our lives, we also need discrimination with regard to claims based on demonstrations of power.

245 Does the fullness of the Holy Spirit imply an increase in our measure of spiritual gift?

Not necessarily. It means rather that there will be a more effective use of whatever measure of gift we have. A one-talent person does not necessarily become a five-talent person because he is filled with the Spirit. But he will be able to make full use of his one talent, under God. This is not to say he may not receive additional gifts as he progresses in life, but this lies within the sovereign will of God. The fullness of the Holy Spirit makes us available instruments to God, enabling Him to work in and through us by His divine power. It is this type of activity which bears fruit for eternity. It is useless to seek the fullness of divine power in our work if we are not filled with the Spirit in our life and character.

What Is Meant by Being "Filled with the Spirit"?

246 The Bible commands us to be filled with the Spirit: does this involve His dwelling in us?

This command is found in Ephesians 5:18: "Be not drunk with wine, wherein is excess, but be filled with the Spirit." It is based on the fact, stated earlier in the epistle (1:13), that the Holy Spirit indwells every believer in Christ: ". . . in whom also, after that ye believed [i.e., having believed], ye were sealed with that holy Spirit of promise." This seal is the indwelling presence of the Holy Spirit which was promised by the Lord Jesus when He said, "I will pray the Father, and he shall give you another Comforter, that he may abide with you forever; even the Spirit of truth; whom the world cannot receive, because it seeth him not, neither knoweth him: but ye know him; for he dwelleth with you, and shall be in you" (Jn 14:16-17).

It was characteristic of the relationship with God of Old Testament believers that the Holy Spirit came upon various individuals, empowering them for special service for the Lord. In the case of some this seemed almost continuous, but it was not the equivalent of the New Testament experience of having the Holy Spirit dwelling within us. Hence it was that when David sinned, part of his prayer of repentance was: "Cast me not away from thy presence; and take not thy holy spirit from me" (Ps 51:11).

Does this mean that David feared he would lose his salvation?   247

We do not see any suggestion of that in the entire passage. But he was keenly aware that his communion with God was broken, and he had no assurance that he would be restored to God's service. At that time the indwelling presence of the Holy Spirit was not the distinguishing mark of a true believer as it is today. It was this to which the Lord Jesus refers in John 14. He states what had been the former relationship and then promises that in the coming dispensation there would be a far more personal relationship, in that the Holy Spirit would indwell every believer. In his first epistle John wrote: "Hereby we know that he abideth in us, by the Spirit which he hath given us" (3:24). There is a similar statement in 4:13. The apostle Paul wrote, in several passages, that the indwelling presence of the Holy Spirit is the seal which guarantees that we belong to God. He adds, in Romans 8:9, "Now if any man have not the Spirit of Christ, he is none of his." This is one of the basic distinctions between the status and privileges of the two dispensations. In this age, based on Christ's advent and His atoning death, resurrection, and ascension into heaven, the Holy Spirit has come into the world with a special ministry not experienced before. The Lord Jesus describes it further in John 16. This ministry so dominates the present age that some have called it "the dispensation of the Holy Spirit," though that term is not found in the Bible.

How does all this relate to our being filled with the Spirit?   248

To be "filled with the Spirit" means not only that we are indwelt by Him, but that He completely pervades our being. This involves certain responsibilities for the way we live. Instead of being repressed by laws administered from without, we are expected to live in self-discipline through the power the Holy Spirit communicates. But this involves what the Bible calls "the communion of the Holy Ghost [Holy Spirit]." We are warned in Ephesians 4:30: "Grieve not the holy Spirit of God, whereby ye are sealed unto the day of redemption." The context indicates that any wrong word, act, or motive grieves the Holy Spirit, and then we are no longer filled with the Spirit. When this occurs, instead of His having free course in our lives and pervading our being, His activity in and through us is "quenched" (1 Th 5:19).

249 What is necessary, then, for us to be "filled with the Spirit"?

A suggestion from D. L. Moody may help us to understand this. He wrote: "If we are to be filled with the Spirit, we must first be emptied of self." This means the yielding of our lives to the control of the Holy Spirit. We can do this by seeking to learn His mind and will and by submitting ourselves to His control and leading. Our most direct and authoritative source of information about the will of God is His Word, the Bible. This Book was written by the inspiration of the Holy Spirit, and as we study it we learn "what is the mind of the Spirit" (Ro 8:27). In fact many students of the Bible consider Colossians 3:16 to be a parallel passage to Ephesians 5:18. The one tells us to be "filled with the Spirit," while the other instructs us: "Let the word of Christ dwell in you richly in all wisdom." It is only in this way that we receive spiritual empowerment for fruitful service for Christ. Instead of living for self-gratification (whatever form that may take) we live to please our Saviour and the Holy Spirit whom He has given. This involves prayer, as well as Bible study, allowing God to communicate His mind through His Word, under the guidance of the Holy Spirit. It also involves sharing the blessings of Christianity with others, since part of the declared will of God is that we should "preach the gospel to every creature" and be witnesses to Him wherever we go (Mk 16:15; Ac 1:8).

250 If one is filled with the Spirit at a given time, can this condition change?

Yes, we can lose the close communion and complete submission to God, but this state can also be recovered and renewed. Our being saved and consequently indwelt by the Holy Spirit is a once-for-all experience. But our being *filled* with the Spirit and having His power in our lives can fluctuate. Hence it is something to be cultivated and safeguarded. The tense of the command implies this, and some translate Ephesians 5:18, "Be *being filled* with the Spirit." By this is meant that we cannot rest on the achievement of such an experience. It must be renewed daily, and perhaps more often. It requires living in the constant consciousness of what we are told in 1 Corinthians 6:19-20: "Know ye not that your body is the temple of the Holy Ghost which is in you, which ye have of God, and ye are not your own? For ye are bought with a price: therefore glorify God in your body, and in your spirit, which are God's." This is not a burdensome kind of existence but rather the opposite. While it will inhibit the indulgence of carnal and wrong desires, it will, on the other hand, open to us the floodgates of God's blessing and His guidance and strength.

PROPHECY

What Is Meant by the Great Tribulation?

251 When the Bible speaks of the "great tribulation" does it mean a time of particular stress, like a death in the family or a heavy loss of some kind; or what does it mean?

It is not simply a time of unusual distress. This has been a world of trouble ever since the advent of sin. Genesis 3 tells us of God's temporary judgment upon sin, bringing a law of physical death on man and putting a curse on the ground so that it brings forth thorns and thistles, making agriculture difficult. There are times of special distress, such as droughts, floods and the like, and epidemics among men, and other disasters. All of these intensify the sorrow of men, and should teach man both his dependence on God and his sinfulness in God's sight. Instead it hardens some so that they blaspheme a God who could permit such conditions to exist; while others, because of seasons of comparative freedom from scourges, think that these are mere accidents of nature, and they do not recognize the hand of God at all.

The Bible teaches that God has a controversy with men because of their rejection of His Son. Many have wondered why, if Jesus were really the Son of God, God did not do something about the rejection and crucifixion of Jesus. The Bible teaches that God will vindicate His Son and the process will be far more drastic than most would expect. Shortly before His crucifixion Jesus referred to this dealing of God, using language similar to that of Daniel the prophet, uttered several centuries before. Christ said, "For then shall be great tribulation, such as was not since the beginning of the world to this time, no, nor ever shall be" (Mt 24:21). This is the "great tribulation."

172

Why has God not brought this time of tribulation before this? 252

It is all part of God's overall dealing with men. Were God to have dealt with our first parents in the fullness of His judgment, it would have meant their immediate execution and eternal doom. Had He purposed to do that, it is unlikely that He would have made man at all. Instead, though God foresaw the sin of man, He planned to hold His judgment in partial abeyance, giving men an opportunity to repent of their sin and turn to Him for salvation. There seems good reason to believe that Adam and Eve, as well as many millions since then, availed themselves of this provision of God's grace. But in order to permit this it was necessary for man to be free to exercise his power of choice. So the world has progressed from one generation to another: not free from the effects of sin, but yet not experiencing the full fruits of it. God causes some of the effects of sin to be apparent now, while other effects will follow in eternity for those who do not receive His salvation.

Why could not the present condition of things go on forever? 253

Because the longsuffering of God is tempered by His holiness, which limits its duration. We read in Genesis 6:3: "The Lord said, My spirit shall not always strive with man." Acts 17:30-31 tells us that God has appointed the day when He shall bring His judgment on man. Several scriptures refer to man's filling up his cup of iniquity, as though God has set an ultimate limit beyond which man may not go. God's tolerance is great but not infinite. When the point is reached where God considers that mankind has committed itself to unbelief, He will make that move which signals the end of this dispensation and the beginning of the great tribulation. The event which signals the change is what is commonly called the rapture, or snatching away, of the Church (1 Th 4:13-18).

This event will be a display of divine power such as the world has never seen, and it will produce some startling changes. The resulting circumstances are described symbolically in Revelation 6-19. Many persons have applied these chapters to various events in history or to current happenings. We believe this view is erroneous, and it has caused many to discredit this portion of Holy Scripture. But we believe these judgments will be visited upon men, causing a time of chaos in human relations, augmented by catastrophic judgments from God. Even during that period God will receive those who come to Him in humility and faith, as He does now; and Scripture states that many will do so. However then, as now, the majority will not submit themselves to God.

254 Do these judgments fall upon all the inhabitants of the earth alike?

In one sense, yes, but for varying purposes. First Corinthians 10:32 divides humanity into three groups from a religious viewpoint: the Jew, the Gentile, and the Church of God; and Scripture indicates that God has a controversy with each. Several of the Jewish prophets foretold these judgments for that nation. We read: "Alas! for that day is great, so that none is like it: it is even the time of Jacob's trouble; but he shall be saved out of it" (Jer 30:7). Other references are Amos 5:18-20 and Zephaniah 1:14-18, for example. But since Jew and Gentile were united in the rejection of Jesus as God's Son, God will deal with Gentile nations also in this coming time of tribulation. We have one description of this in Joel 3:9-16, which specifies the Gentile nations as being the subjects of that prophecy. The book of Revelation also shows that the Gentile nations will share to the full in these coming judgments.

255 Will the Church not be included, since it is mentioned as one of the divisions of humanity in 1 Corinthians 10:32?

It is our understanding that true believers in Christ will be caught up to heaven before this time begins. But many who profess church membership have never personally submitted themselves to Him in the obedience of faith. The Lord's message to the church at Sardis speaks of many who have a name to live but who are dead (Rev 3:1). These are not members of the true Church which constitutes the spiritual body of Christ (Eph 1:22-23). It is common in church circles today to hear the Bible denied, and in some cases every foundation truth of Christianity is rejected. Some think the Lord's message to Thyatira, contained in Revelation 2:21-22, threatens such persons with being left to share in this tribulation judgment. The references to fornication and adultery in that passage are to be taken in a spiritual sense, though the physical sins may be present also. Let us make sure that we have personally taken our stand on the Lord's side, acknowledging Him as our Lord and Saviour.

What Is Armageddon?

We hear much about "the battle of Armageddon." What does this mean, and where did the term originate? 256

The term is found in the Bible, in Revelation 16, where we read of a great gathering of nations for a military conflict just prior to Christ's second advent. It is called "the battle of that great day of God Almighty" (v. 14), and verse 16 says, "And he gathered them together into a place called in the Hebrew tongue Armageddon." This is a transliteration of the Hebrew *Har Megiddo*, which means "mountain of a multitude," or "mountain of rendezvous." It is the name given the final world conflict before Christ's return to earth. Some have suggested as a translation of the term *mountain of slaughter*, but perhaps this is by implication. That there will be a great slaughter of men is evident, for Ezekiel 39:9 says one result of it will be that the inhabitants of the land will have firewood from the implements of war to last them several years. Verse 12 states that it will require seven months to bury the dead. The Lord Jesus Christ said that if those days were not shortened no one would be spared (Mt 24:22).

Who will be involved in that war, and what will be the outcome of it? 257

It will be a war of global proportions, and if there is not another world war in the meantime, it would be World War III, on a grander scale than anything which has preceded it. Scripture indicates that the great powers of the North and East will be on the one side, and those of the West on the other. Revelation 9:16

speaks of an army of 200 million men. It seems incredible that such an army could be amassed, even granting that it includes the supply services, reserves, etc., yet John adds: "and I heard the number of them," much as we might say, "You heard me aright."

This host is identified with the North and East in various ways. Revelation 9:14-15 shows us that they are released from the River Euphrates "for to slay the third part of men." In 16:12 we are told of the River Euphrates being dried up "that the way of the kings of the east might be prepared." It is literally, "the kings from the sun rising." Since Japan is known as the land of the sunrise, this may very well include them; and some think India will also be in this coalition of nations. Another verse which helps to identify this enormous horde is Daniel 11:44, where we read of the great leader being troubled by tidings "out of the east and out of the north." This joining of North and East suggests that whatever conflict of interest or ideology there may be now between Russia and China may be resolved, and in this great struggle the army of 200 million men might be drawn from the combined populations of Russia, China, Japan, and possibly India.

258 What part will the United States have in this conflict?

Several expositors have noted that the prophetic Scriptures do not anywhere speak of a great military power in the West. We read of the King of the North, the King of the South, and the powers of the East, but not of a great power in the West, particularly the Far West. It should be understood that the prophets were Israelites, and their statements regarding direction contemplated Palestine as the point of reference. This is appropriate, since Palestine is declared to be the center from which Christ will govern the earth. But the description of the events of the last days gives no suggestion of their being influenced by any great power in the West.

It may be argued that the United States did not exist as a nation when these prophecies were given, but this would not account for the omission if there will be a powerful nation here at that time. In the prophecies of Daniel mention is made of Greece as a coming dominant power long before that country was unified into a nation. And even if the United States were not named, there could easily have been some description of such a power in this geographical area. We know of none.

It may be of interest that some expositors, writing before the turn of the century, concluded that since there was no mention in prophecy of any great power in the West, it could be that the United States, which rose to power very quickly, might subside as quickly, and that there would therefore be no great power in the West at the time of the end. One of these writers, at least, without claiming divine authority for his opinion, ventured the guess that this might come about, not necessarily by an attack from without but perhaps by internal strife and anarchy. A similar opinion was offered from a purely secular research by Lord Macauley, the essayist and student of history and government. It was his opinion that the very elements which made our government strong in the days when we had to struggle for survival would work for our political disintegration when we achieved an opulent society.

In the light of prophecy, could any of the current military con- 259
frontations be considered the beginning of this final conflict?

Only in the sense of a preparatory groundwork. God often works through seemingly natural events to bring about certain conditions. Current events might serve to break certain political and social ties, thus leading to changes in national affiliations, which could eventuate in the coalitions which prophecy foretells. But Scripture also foretells other events which could bring all this about; so, it does not follow that any current political movement is prophetically significant. If we are at or near the time of the end, as many believe, though none can be certain, then the one place where political and military confrontation could have future significance is the land of Palestine. Scripture concerns itself not so much with the relationships of governments among themselves as with God's dealings with men. Since this, from the time of Abraham, has been centered in the nation which sprang from him, anything affecting their welfare is likely to have prophetical significance, but only if we are at the time when God is about to bring that nation back into the place of His favor, as Paul foretells in his parable of the olive tree (Ro 11). The apostle speaks of

God's putting the natural branches back into their original place, and this will signal the movement of God to bring to fulfillment the prophecies concerning the millennial kingdom of Christ.

Will the Nation of Israel Survive?

260 In view of the animosities between the Israelis and their neighboring Arabic nations, can the nation of Israel survive?

Israel as a people should be distinguished from Israel as a nation, though the Word of God speaks of both. The survival of Israel as a people has been a striking fulfillment of Hosea 3:4: "For the children of Israel shall abide many days without a king, and without a prince, and without a sacrifice, and without an image, and without an ephod, and without teraphim." That is to say, the people would survive as an identifiable ethnic group even though for many days (which have lengthened into many centuries) they would be without any political or religious center for the group. They have been merged into the political and social structures of many nations, and yet have not been absorbed as is usually the case with mixed nationalities. It was this fact that caused the chaplain at the court of the king of Prussia to give his famous reply to the question, "Could you give proof, in a word, that the Bible is true?" His reply: The Jew.

The Bible also speaks of the eventual establishment of Israel as a nation, and declares that it will be the chief of the nations, and that in the millennial kingdom of Christ Jerusalem will be the political and religious capital of the world. However, this does not assure the permanence of the present national structure. God may see fit to preserve this structure, and many think He will do so, but the prophecies of the Bible do not require that it must be preserved.

261 It has been taught by some that the establishment of Israel as a nation in 1948 was in fulfillment of Bible prophecy. Is this correct?

It was clearly *not* the fulfillment of those prophecies which assign to Israel the place of leadership to which we have alluded.

Her very existence has been precarious from the start, and in spite of their startling military success in the six-day war in 1967, their existence as a nation is still under threat. In fact, the Word of God itself suggests two aspects of their establishment as a nation. Besides their establishment as the head of the nations, as in Isaiah 2:1-4, there is also a less noticed prophecy in Ezekiel which speaks of their being gathered for judgment. In the nature of things, this must precede the other.

Ezekiel, in 22:19-22, after describing the refining of precious metals in crucible fires, speaks of God gathering His people Israel in like manner. "Yea, I will gather you," He says, "and blow upon you in the fire of my wrath, and ye shall be melted in the midst thereof. As silver is melted in the midst of the furnace, so shall ye be melted in the midst thereof." This might be considered to have had its fulfillment in the trials of Israel in the days of Antiochus Epiphanes, or later when the Romans destroyed Jerusalem. But this and similar prophecies, while having a partial fulfillment in the past, seem to have also a future outlook, preparatory to God's complete restoration of Israel to a place of higher glory than she has ever known in the past.

Are there not other prophecies being fulfilled now, such as the 262
desert blossoming as a rose? Does this not indicate that we have
reached the time when we may expect the fulfillment of the prom-
ise of Israel's glory?

In our understanding of Scripture, we do not believe specific prophecies are being fulfilled at present, though current events do produce some similarities. Desert places in Palestine are being made to blossom by means of irrigation. But the prophecies in Isaiah 35 include the healing of physical ailments as well as the rejuvenation of nature, and we are told elsewhere in the Bible that this will be due to the lifting of the curse of sin from the earth. (See Ro 8:19-25.) This refers to what happened in Genesis 3:17-19. When this is reversed it will not be fruitfulness due to weeding and irrigation, but all will be accomplished and sustained by the power of God. "Instead of the thorn shall come up the fir tree, and instead of the briar shall come up the myrtle tree: and it shall be to the LORD for a name, for an everlasting sign that shall not be cut off" (Is 55:13). This condition does not prevail today.

263 What are some of the prophecies of Israel's future place among the nations?

These are too numerous to give anything like a list. One that is repeated, almost verbatim, is found in Isaiah 2:2-4, and Micah 4:1-3. The description is often quoted as the ideal in human relations: "They shall beat their swords into plowshares, and their spears into pruning hooks: nation shall not lift up sword against nation, neither shall they learn war any more" (Is 2:4). At that time this prophecy tells us that "Out of Zion shall go forth the law, and the word of the Lord from Jerusalem" (Is 2:3). This is saying that at that time Jerusalem and Mount Zion will be the capital of the world, the political center. The law will be promulgated there, and any direct revelation from God will originate there. Then will be fulfilled the promise of Deuteronomy 28:13, "The Lord shall make thee the head, and not the tail; and thou shalt be above only, and thou shalt not be beneath; if that thou hearken unto the commandments of the Lord thy God. . . ." This is not a prophecy, but it promises that if they were obedient, they should find themselves at the head of the nations. The nearest approach to such a condition was in Solomon's day, but this fell very far short of God's ideal for them. It will find its fulfillment in the millennium.

In a different setting, Zechariah 14:16-17 states, "And it shall come to pass that every one that is left of all the nations which came against Jerusalem, shall even go up from year to year to worship the King, the LORD of hosts, and to keep the feast of tabernacles. And it shall be, that whoso will not come up of all the families of the earth unto Jerusalem to worship the King, the LORD of hosts, even upon them shall be no rain." We see from this that Jerusalem will also be the religious center of the world.

264 Should we as Christians work for the establishment of the Jewish state?

These things are presented in Scripture as being accomplished by the power of God, and their fulfillment is dependent on the second advent of Christ. While the conmmand to "Pray for the peace of Jerusalem" (Ps 122:6) does not strictly belong to this dispensation, I am sure many Christians have both the material and spiritual welfare of Israel on their hearts, as well as that of other nations. But our commission is to preach the gospel to every creature. In Bible times social and political benefits were the result of spiritual transformation. To make political systems our major concern would not only distract us from our primary thrust, but would also involve cooperation with some persons who are not at all seeking God's will, but rather personal advantage. They may be motivated by patriotism, but its objective is not necessarily related to the Word and will of God.

Is the United States Mentioned in Prophecy?

**We often hear discussions of the place of various countries in   265
prophecy. Is the United States mentioned in prophecy?**

Not directly, if at all. We have often observed that various nations are mentioned in the Bible as they relate to the nation of Israel. The account of creation and all of human history down to the time of Abraham is comprised in the first eleven chapters of the Bible. The rest of the fifty chapters of Genesis are devoted to the record of Abraham and his posterity, down to his great-grandson Joseph. Throughout the Bible, both in its history and prophecy, the central theme is God's dealing with His people, the descendants of Abraham. While God is concerned with every member of the human race, yet He has not given us the history of any other of the peoples of the earth.

We believe this observation is confirmed by the statement in Deuteronomy 32:8, "When the Most High divided to the nations their inheritance, when he separated the sons of Adam, he set the bounds of the people according to the number of the children of Israel." If this refers to the dispersion of the peoples of the earth following the attempt to build the tower of Babel, it would mean that this was done on the basis of God's foreknowledge.

That is to say, in the original arrangement of the races which developed out of the families of the three sons of Noah, God ordained that Israel should be in a strategic position, though being themselves one of the smallest ethnic groups. Prophecy indicates that the land of Israel will be the scene of the final struggle between the nations seeking to establish themselves in political and military dominance in the earth.

266 How does this relate to the United States and the Americas?

With regard to Bible history, the United States, of course, did not exist as a nation in Bible times, though there were nations of aboriginal peoples in both North and South America, some with a highly developed civilization even at that time. But since they had no relationship with Israel, they are not mentioned in the Bible. With regard to prophecy, though we have numerous details of events and nations to be involved in the last days, we know of no direct reference to any great power in the west participating in the struggles which will culminate in Armageddon. It seems unlikely, as others have remarked, that one of the greatest military powers of all time should be omitted from direct mention if it were to have a part in the events immediately preceding the establishment of Christ's kingdom on earth. For this reason we assume that the United States will not be a prominent factor, if it participates at all, in those events.

267 Would it be possible for the United States to remain aloof from what is portrayed as a worldwide struggle of the major nations of the earth?

It does not seem likely, if the United States were to remain a great military power until that time. Some scholars have, for various reasons, questioned whether the United States *will remain* a dominant military and political factor in the world affairs. The late Joseph Stalin once remarked that "History shows there are no invincible armies." This is another way of saying that no nation has continued indefinitely as a dominant military power. Some

have been of comparatively short duration, as the empire of
Napoleon. Others, as the Roman Empire, and that of Great
Britain, have been of greater duration. Thomas Babington Macauley, writing more than a century ago, as a student of political
science, ventured the thought that the United States' form of government was of such a nature that it would not endure. He felt
that the very elements which made our nation strong in times of
danger, and when life was largely a struggle for existence, would
make us weak once security and affluence were achieved. Life
would then cease to be a matter of survival, and would become a
struggle to obtain a greater share of the wealth produced from an
abundance of natural resources. He did not, of course, foresee
how greatly the recently developed technology would augment
this; but history has borne out his observation. He felt that this
could readily lead to the disintegration of the nation into an in-
ternationally helpless community, whose members would live in
social alienation from one another.

Does this view deny any prophetical implications about the 268
United States found in the Bible?

We believe not. Some have felt that the woman who rides the
beast in Revelation 17, called "Babylon the great," may represent
apostate Christendom. Many persons are Christian in name who
do not have the inward conviction of faith in Christ which makes
them true disciples of Him, and who have never experienced the
new birth. Such persons are not acknowledged in the Bible as
members of the church which Christ is building (Mt 16:18).
These will be left in the world when true believers are caught up
at the coming of Christ, portrayed in 1 Thessalonians 4:13-18.
Organizationally this might represent a strong group, scattered
throughout various countries, and this group may well have a
prominent part in establishing the government represented by the
"beast."

Some who hold this view have thought that wherever there is a
considerable number of persons who would be considered "Christian" in contrast with other world religions, but who do not pro-

fess personal faith in Christ, these would be included in "Babylon
the great." It is thought that many persons in the United States
and other countries of North and South America fall into this
category, placing them within the scope of this prophecy. But
even if we accept this identification it does not necessarily follow
that the western nations will be involved politically or militarily
in the events described in Revelation 9 to 16. Hence their con-
tinuance as world powers is not necessary to any prophetical implication found in the Bible.

**269 Have others besides Lord Macauley predicted or suggested the
demise of the United States as a world power?**

Yes. The late William Kelly, a widely known Bible expositor,
writing also about a century ago, made a similar suggestion on
purely biblical grounds. He speaks of the United States being
composed of heterogeneous elements from various nations, some
of high caliber, but others of baser character. "So I believe," he
wrote, "they will break up into factions of noisy primitive elements; and . . . will at length burst as a bubble." He remarks
that "Population does not in itself make a nation strong," and he
cites the conquest of great nations by smaller and seemingly in-
consequential groups. "So as to America," he adds, "I conceive
that the young giant power which has grown so fast will sink
still faster, probably through intestine quarrel, but assuredly
somehow before that day comes. They will break up into different fragments. . . . For it is a remarkable fact that there is no
place in prophecy for the vast influential power, such as the
American United States would be, if it so long retained cohesion."
Perhaps his opinion may be given greater weight from the fact
that on the same page he states his belief that Britain would lose
India, and he speaks of immense success which Russia would
attain. At the time he wrote, neither of these seemed likely. He
also spoke of the final judgment of all the enemies of God. We
believe the suggestions mentioned may well be within the mind
of God, since Scripture does not make any specific reference to
the United States so far as we know.

Do Gog and Magog Represent Russia?

**The book of Ezekiel speaks of Gog and the land of Magog. I   270
have heard this refers to Russia. Is there any ground for this?**

Yes, there is some ground for it, but we do not believe the identification is conclusive. In fact, it is very precarious. Ezekiel 38:2
says, "Son of man, set thy face against Gog, the land of Magog,
the chief prince of Meshech and Tubal, and prophesy against
him." Verse 3 also identifies Gog as "the chief prince of Meshech
and Tubal." The expression *chief prince* is translated by some,
"prince of Rosh." The similarity between this and Russia is en-
hanced by the similarity between Meshech and Tubal, and Mos-
cow and Tobolsk, two cities of Russia. This makes it easy to
identify Gog and Magog with Russia. There may be some substance to this identification, but it would have to be on a broader
base than similarity of names.

The name Gog does not occur other than in Ezekiel 38 and 39,
and in Revelation 20:8, except for an otherwise unidentified person in the genealogy of Reuben in 1 Chronicles 5:4. However,
the name Magog goes back to the days of Noah. Genesis 10:2
gives the name Magog as being that of the second son of Japheth,
the son of Noah. Interestingly, the names Tubal and Meshech
also occur in the list of descendants of Japheth, as do Gomer and
Togarmah, mentioned in Ezekiel 38:6. With five of the names in
Ezekiel 38 occurring in the list of the sons of Japheth (one a
grandson) we feel there is solid ground for assuming that whatever else may be involved, the identification here is with the descendants of Japheth.

Is there any way of knowing what geographical area is involved?   271

We believe it can be known in a general way, but not precisely.
Besides the names given, the expression "many people" occurs
several times in this passage. We assume, therefore, that the
prophecy relates to a coalition of peoples, whose general location
is said to be "the north quarters" (Eze 38:6, 15; 39:2). It must be
remembered that in the Bible, directions relate to the land of
Palestine. In the prophecies of Daniel 11 the kings of the north

were those of the territory of Syria, while those of the south were
the kings of Egypt. However, the nations of Assyria and Babylon
were also said to have come down from the north. But we do not
know of any Scripture which limits the expression to what we
might call Palestine's "near north," and in a quite different prophecy in Jeremiah 25:26 there is mention of "all the kings of the
north, far and near." This is broad enough to include the far
north, which would be Russia, though not excluding the closer
nations to the north of Israel. Their troubles in the past seem to
have come more from the north than from any other direction,
though not exclusively so.

272 How are Gog and Magog related? Can they be defined?

Not precisely. Ezekiel 38:3 identifies Gog as the prince, as do
also other references to him in chapters 38 and 39. While Magog
is the name of a person in Genesis 10, it seems here to refer to
the land from which they come. Revelation 20:8, while speaking
of an entirely different time, joins Gog and Magog together, and
seems to relate both names to the land. But Genesis 10 clearly
identifies the names with the descendants of Japheth, whether
we think of land or people.

While the distribution of the human race is not precisely recorded, it would appear that the descendants of Japheth spread
out over a wide area of the earth, and it appears that a considerable segment of these descendants are to come down from the
north, quite possibly including the far north. This would include
Russia, and also the nearer territories to the north of Israel in Asia
Minor and southeastern Europe. Other prophecies speak of an
invasion also from the east, while Daniel's "seventy weeks" prophecy indicates that the western powers will support the nation on
the basis of a seven-year covenant to be consummated at the
beginning of the tribulation period.

**273 Ezekiel 38 speaks of these enemies of Israel coming down (or "go-
ing up") to "the land of unwalled villages." Can we know the time
and circumstances referred to?**

There is considerable difference of view among scholars as to
this. It would not be possible within a limited scope to discuss the

various views in detail. Some think it will take place a considerable time after the millennial kingdom of Christ is set up, yet prior
to the very end of that time. This seems to me incongruous with
the other prophecies which relate to that period. My own understanding is rather that Israel will become "a land of unwalled villages" (that is, "open country," as we speak in these days) because they will rely on the western powers with whom they will
have a security pact, mentioned in Daniel 9:27. I take it that this
pact will assure territorial integrity, as well as freedom of religion.
Daniel speaks of this pact being broken in the middle of the specified time of seven years. Revelation 13 gives some additional
details concerning this.

Somewhere during this period will occur this invasion, as I understand it, which will eventuate in Armageddon. We take this to
be, not a single battle, but a *war* in which the western powers
defend Israel, not on any religious basis, but on purely political
and military considerations. The northern powers will be the in-
vaders, and apparently, from Revelation 9 and 16, the eastern
powers will invade at the same time. Whether this will be in
coalition with the northern powers, or with motives and objec-
tives of their own is not entirely clear. The true believers in the
Lord Jesus at that time will not constitute an organized group, but
will be "underground." Apparently there will be a group of these
with whom some false prophets will establish contact, endeavor-
ing to lure them from their place of hiding (Mt 24:26-27). It
appears that the active witness for Christ will be during the first
half of that seventieth week of Daniel. In the last half it will rest
largely with the two witnesses of Revelation 11.

**What is the relation between what is said of Gog and Magog in 274
Ezekiel 38 and 39, and what is stated in Revelation 20?**

Revelation 20 is a most interesting prophecy, since it shows that
even after a thousand years of the beneficent reign of Christ, mul-
titudes of people will still prefer the liberty to sin. When Satan
is loosed from the abyss temporarily he will have no trouble in
gathering a host of people to follow him in rebellion against
Christ. Unlike the disobedience of man in the garden of Eden,
this time the judgment of God will be swift and sure, followed

immediately by the Great White Throne judgment, meting out
to the lost their eternal doom.

The use of the names of Gog and Magog in this chapter may be
intended to show a similarity with the war against Palestine prior
to the millennium. They indicate widely scattered peoples, at a
distance from Palestine. This shows the incorrigibility of sin,
which can only be forgiven on the ground of the atonement of
Christ, and can only be overcome through the regenerating power
of the Holy Spirit.

Does China Figure in Prophecy?

275 **Since China has so vast a population, and now sophisticated
weaponry, giving that country a tremendous potential for influ-
encing the affairs of the world, should we not expect that it would
have prominent mention in the prophecies of Scripture?**

On the basis of human reasoning we might think so, but it is
interesting that both in Bible history and prophecy God is not
concerned with giving us a detailed account of the acts or achieve-
ments of men. Essentially the Bible is an account of the dealings
of God with His people. The first 11 chapters of Genesis cover
the whole of human history (including creation itself) up to the
time of Abraham. Chapters 12 through 50 give us God's account
of the life of Abraham down to the death of his great-grandson
Joseph. This suggests the comparative importance which God
places on the events of history. Likewise throughout the Old
Testament other nations are mentioned as they have some relation, whether close or remote, with the nation of Israel.

Since the Chinese had no direct relations with the nation of
Israel, we have no account of that people, even though they had a
highly developed civilization in Bible times. Even the great
civilizations of Assyria, Egypt, and Babylon get relatively scant
mention, and what is given is because of their contact with or influence on the history of Israel. The oriental civilizations and the
cultures of the Americas are not mentioned at all. The great ad-
vances in science, art, and architecture in ancient times are amaz-

ing. Medical science was so advanced that it is believed that cataract operations were common in the days of Hammurabi, and that the Incas practiced some form of brain surgery before the time of Christ. Ancient temples and other structures are marvels of art and architecture. Yet the Bible says nothing of all this.

Is China mentioned at all in the Bible?   276

There is one passage in the Bible which may possibly refer to China, though this is not certain. Isaiah 49:12 says, "Behold, these shall come from far: and, lo, these from the north and from the west; and these from the land of Sinim." The land of Sinim would seem to be in the East, and the word bears a remarkable resemblance to the word used for China, especially in a combining form, as in Sino-Soviet relations. The word could, however, refer to an entirely different area, so we cannot be sure of its application.

Does this mean that China will have no place in the events pre- 277 ceding Christ's coming, because it is not mentioned in prophecy?

This does not necessarily follow, since, though China is not mentioned directly, it seems to be included in certain general descriptions of the powers which will be active in the last days. Were China to have direct national relations with Israel it would undoubtedly be mentioned separately. Since the contact will be part of.a larger combination of forces it does not require separate identification. If the reference in Isaiah 49:12 is actually to China, it would show that this nation has not been overlooked.

What place will China have in the last days? What are some of 278 the indirect references?

There are two references in Revelation which seem to include the people of China. Revelation 16:12 speaks of a judgment which follows the pouring out of a vial by the sixth of seven angels who are instrumental in bringing forth the judgments of God at that time. He is said to pour out his vial "upon the great river Euphrates." The prophecy adds, "And the water thereof was dried up, that the way of the kings of the east might be

prepared." The word used for *east* signifies the rising of the sun,
which we usually attach to the far east. There is a parallel statement in chapter 9 in connection with the blowing of the sixth
trumpet. The river Euphrates is mentioned there also (v. 14),
in connection with an army of "two hundred thousand thousand"
(v. 16). This would be two hundred million. Numbers in the
Bible are not always precise, and the wording here is "two
myriads of myriads." We could not insist on the precise figure
of two hundred million, but since John immediately adds: "And
I heard the number of them," it could be that this figure is the
one intended.

If this be accepted, it could very well be that the combined
forces of the Orient (not "somewhere east of Suez," but east of
the Euphrates) will be involved in this judgment. This could
include the combined forces of China, Japan, and India. These
countries could, conceivably, form an Asian pact, and from other
prophecies it would appear that they will act in collaboration
with the northern powers, including Russia, because the northern powers are said to descend on Jerusalem at the same time as
these powers attack from the east. In the Bible geographical
areas are described by their location relative to the land of
Israel.

**279 What will be the end of China? If it is not mentioned directly in
the Bible, can we know what its future will be?**

If we refer to its immediate future, the answer is No. We cannot foretell the progression of events between now and the time
when the prophecies concerning the coming tribulation will
begin to be fulfilled. The present political setup of the world
could be the basis for the fulfillment of prophecy, should the
rapture of the church take place. On the other hand, should that
event not take place for some time, there might be some important
realignments of nations. The possibilities include a possible
World War III before the Lord comes, though the Bible does
not predict this before the rapture of the church.

But at the end of the tribulation period, the Lord Jesus Christ
will set up a kingdom on earth, when "the earth shall be full of
the knowledge of the Lord, as the waters cover the sea" (Is

11:9). All nations will be required to come up to Jerusalem yearly to observe certain feast days, and to worship "the King, the LORD of hosts" (Zech 14:17). At that time the kingdoms of the world shall have become the kingdoms of our Lord and of His Christ (Rev 11:15). This will include China, Russia, and all other nations. If the United States still exists at that time it will have a part in this also. The word *king* is used of a ruler, whether officially called a king or not. The holy city Jerusalem will be the capital both of Israel, and of the world, and we are told that the kings of the earth shall bring their glory and honor into it or, unto it (Rev 21:24). But we do not believe we can apply these prophetical truths to current events. These conditions will be effected by the second advent of Christ to the earth. In the meantime we have no certain assurance as to what course current political developments will take. It is the final result that is assured.

CHRISTIAN ETHICS

What Does the Bible Say About Birth Control?

280 Why are there so many conflicting views about birth control? Does the Bible speak on this subject?

The only seemingly direct reference to this subject in the Bible is the case of Onan (Gen 38:8-10). He did not use a contraceptive but refused to consummate copulation. In this reference it is not clear whether it was this which was considered sinful in itself or whether the sin lay in his refusal to fulfill the law of levirate marriage. This law required that if a man died childless a surviving brother should marry the widow, and the first child was considered to be the deceased's and to be his heir. The context shows that this was an established practice at that time, and later a similar provision was written into the Mosaic code. Since there is no definitive statement in the Bible on the subject of birth control, one's views must be arrived at by considering the implications of other truths.

281 What are some of the truths which bear on this subject?

One is the purpose of marriage. There are those who consider this to be solely the propagation of the human race; but while this is one of its chief purposes, we do not believe it is the only one. In the beginning, instead of creating a community, God created a single person, a man; and from the man God formed a woman, so that the two shared a common life. While in one sense the human race was created in the first man, yet God so ordered the circumstances that we should come into being one by one and generation by generation. The bringing forth of children was not the result of sin, as some have supposed, but it is in the nature of man's being. Before sin entered human experience God commanded the man and woman to "be fruitful and multiply, and replenish [or, fill] the earth" (Gen 1:28).

Part of man's commission was to "subdue" the earth, and in the early days of human history large families were highly desirable, especially when, because of man's sin, his work load was increased and there were dangers to be faced, both from man and beast. Children could help with the work necessary to provide sustenance, and men in the family could help guard against danger (Ps 127:3-5). Also there was plenty of space for expansion as new families were formed through the marriage of older children. Conditions in modern times are vastly different in many areas, and it is questionable whether the command given to Adam and Eve is intended to apply.

Are there other considerations which must be taken into account? 282

Yes. Scripture clearly indicates that one of the purposes of marriage is to provide mutual comfort and moral support, apart from the rearing of children. In some cases a married couple finds it impossible to have children, yet their marriage is a blessing to both of them, and there is no suggestion that they should not have normal conjugal relations. In fact, one of the reasons given for marriage is the satisfaction of an overpowering sexual urge. In 1 Corinthians 7:9 Paul says, "It is better to marry than to burn." The context makes it clear that one of the intended purposes of the marriage relationship is to satisfy the sexual urge in a lawful way. It is important to note that the Bible does not sanction the sexual act out of wedlock. Each person is required to "possess his vessel in sanctification and honor" (1 Th 4:4) and to "abstain from fornication" (v. 3).

Why should anyone practice birth control? 283

Many married couples feel they have valid reasons for not having children or at least limiting the number. While this is disapproved in some circles, even the Roman Catholic church, whose official position condemns other forms of birth control, accepts what is called the rhythm method. This involves a measure of abstinence but admittedly condones the principle of having sexual relations only when it is believed they will not result in conception. This seems to me to eliminate the question of morality and to make it a matter of the method one uses. On this basis many feel that the method used is incidental, though conflicting views are held in church circles. Some condemn the use of contraceptives, while others feel it is the duty of parents to limit the size of their families to the number that they can support comfortably and where each can have the maximum benefits of the so-called good life. In all such discussions it must be borne in mind that we are speaking of conjugal relations within the bonds of matrimony. To use contraceptives to prevent conception out of wedlock is simply to augment the sin of such a relationship.

284 Are there any considerations for not practicing birth control?

Yes. It does not necessarily follow that life on a high economic and social level is best. One has known persons whose lives have been blighted by receiving too much too soon, without effort, achieving, or deserving. Often such persons never develop the moral fiber or purpose in life which others gain through the struggle necessitated by poverty or difficult conditions and privation. Man has inward spiritual needs which are not met by material benefits. Often it is in the very struggles against adversity that a person develops the latent strengths and gains the insights which give the satisfaction of achievement. Without such development there is often frustration and aimlessness which leads to a destructive outlook and fosters delinquency.

Often parents of large families feel that their children are a trust from the Lord and love between parents and children is fostered and deepened by mutual dependence. Frequently older children help care for younger ones, and the burdens are not as great as might be assumed; and these responsibilities help the children to mature and develop their own talents, making them more useful members of society. History shows that geniuses and great leaders have sometimes been later members of large families. Benjamin Franklin's father had seventeen children, of whom Benjamin was the fifteenth, the youngest of the sons. John Wesley made a tremendous spiritual impact on the world. His godly and capable mother was herself a late arrival in a very large family, and she bore her husband nineteen children of whom John was the fifteenth and his brother Charles, whose numerous hymns have been a blessing to so many, was the last. Who can measure the blessing brought to humanity by these two brothers who owed their existence, under God, to parents willing to have so large a family?

Does the Bible Condemn Abortion?

Does the Bible say anything about abortion, and if so, does it con- 285 **demn it?**

As with many other subjects the teaching of the Bible concerning this question must be gained indirectly. We must consider not only the "spirit" of the Bible but also the implications of its teaching on related subjects. While the Bible does not speak directly about abortion, it has much to say about the taking of life, which is declared to be the prerogative of God and only to be done by men on divine authority. "Whoso sheddeth man's blood, by man shall his blood be shed" (Gen 9:6). The Bible also speaks of God as the Author of life, and as in marriage, "What therefore God hath joined together, let not man put asunder," so it says by implication, "When God has given life, let not man take it away."

We take it, then, that we are to consider what the Bible teaches about the impartation of life and the circumstances under which it may be taken away. Abortion comes under the larger heading of euthanasia. Is it desirable to shorten the life of certain persons, and if so, under what conditions? Just as many consider it right and proper to shorten the life of older persons under certain prescribed conditions, others think it right to prevent children from coming to birth under some conditions.

286   Is abortion in the same category as contraception or birth control?

We believe not. Birth control involves the prevention of conception, while abortion involves the destruction or removal of an embryo or fetus after conception has taken place. Whether we accept birth control or not, it cannot be classified as the destruction of a life already conceived. In coitus most of the spermatozoa are lost in the natural course, and this is not viewed as loss of life. Whether acceptable or not on other terms, contraception does not involve any taking of life.

287   When is a separate life considered to have actually begun?

There are different views of this, the two major ones being called creationism and traducianism. According to creationism God puts a newly created spirit within the person at the time of actual birth and the life is not considered to have been complete until *then* except in its physical constitution. In the other view, when conception takes place there is the transmission of an entire human life—spirit and soul and body. Each view has certain biblical difficulties, but we favor traducianism, inasmuch as we are said to be "in Adam" by our natural birth and "in Christ" by new birth. If we received a separate spirit at birth, we do not see how we could be "by *nature* the children of wrath," as is said in Ephesians 2:3. It would mean that a newly created and thus entirely pure spirit is put in a body transmitted from our first parents, and this would put personality in our body rather than in our spirit.

But traducianism, the transmission of an entire personality through conception, involves there being at conception not only an embryo physical life but a distinct human personality. Hence the taking of life after conception has been established could be considered a form of murder. In this respect it is closely akin to euthanasia.

288   Does the Bible ever permit either abortion or euthanasia?

Here again we must be guided by the implications of Scripture, rather than by any specific statement. With regard to the ending of the life of one who is helpless or suffering, we have, first of all, the command that we are not to kill (Ex 20:13). And though man may think it an act of kindness, it may not prove to have been so in the sight of God. We are not speaking now of prolonging life artificially when the natural processes fail. There may be times when the artificial prolongation of life may not be desirable; but we are speaking of what might be called the artificial shortening of life. It is God our Maker with whom we have to do, and we do not believe the power of life and death rests either in the individual himself or with his relatives or physician. Taking life is quite different from relieving pain by medication which does not vitally affect the life principle which we believe comes from God and is regulated by Him. Some have confused these issues.

In the matter of abortion, there are circumstances which sometimes make it desirable, as when it seems evident to competent medical authority that allowing the life to mature would endanger the life of the mother. Some have taught that in such a case the life of the child should be matured and the life of the mother given up. Where the death of the mother occurs *without design,* it must be accepted, of course, but we do not see in the Bible any authority to plan things that way.

What about abnormal conditions, as when it is believed that the 289 **child will .be abnormal or where conception has resulted from rape, perhaps by a person totally repugnant to the expectant mother for reasons which will involve the offspring as well?**

It would be impossible to discuss in full the ramifications of such a subject. And since the Bible is not explicit, we cannot claim competency to pronounce authoritatively even in a given case. We have tried to explain what is involved: the sovereignty of God in giving life and the fact that He alone is justified in taking it. That God has given certain conditions under which life may be taken indicates that, though life is sacred, this is not absolute in every circumstance of life. In view of this, we do not believe we can condemn abortion without the possibility of exception.

On the other hand to authorize abortion as a form of birth control, or for the convenience of unwed mothers, seems to us a violation of a basic commandment of God. If He has given life by permitting conception to take place, that life is as sacred to Him as that of any person who has been born and who has come to maturity. If we believe there is more to life than our physical being, then we are not at liberty to destroy life except as an agent of God, acting in obedience to His revealed will and taking into consideration the truths of His Word. Abortion solely for convenience disregards God and actually means that man is exercising the divine prerogative. We do not see in the Bible any authorization for such a statute, though, as we have said, we do not believe that abortion should be absolutely prohibited in every circumstance.

What Does the Bible Teach About Racial Intermarriage?

290 Many persons fear that school integration will lead to racial intermarriage: does the Bible say anything on this question?

The Bible for the most part ignores the matter of color divisions in humanity. It recognizes that they exist but does not explain how they came into being. And while it makes reference to certain aspects of the matter, it does so in a casual and factual way. We read, for instance, "Can the Ethiopian change his skin, or the leopard his spots? then may ye also do good, that are accustomed to do evil" (Jer 13:23). This verse neither disparages nor praises the Ethiopian, but it uses him as an example. It simply recognizes the patent fact, without emotional involvement, much as we speak of the rich or the poor.

One text seems designed to show that color differences are not essentially important. I refer to Acts 17:26-27, where we read that God "hath made of one blood all nations of men for to dwell on all the face of the earth, and hath determined the times before appointed, and the bounds of their habitation; that they should seek the Lord, if haply they might feel after him, and find him, though he be not far from every one of us." Many authorities omit the word "blood" and read simply "of one." In either case the ultimate meaning is one source. This emphasizes that the human race is essentially one, springing, in the first instance, from Adam and Eve and later from Noah.

What is the meaning of the clause referring to the bounds of their 291
habitation? Does this mean that God intended the races to remain apart?

We cannot say whether that was God's intention for all time. Prior to the judgment of God upon men in connection with the Tower of Babel (Gen 11), mankind appears to have lived as a unified community. The Scripture statement is that they all had one language, but the circumstances also indicate one community. But at that time God confounded their language, creating separate linguistic communities. It could very well be that divisions were made along other lines also. There appears to have been a time when humanity was actually segregated, so that the yellow race was in Asia, the brown race chiefly on the Asian subcontinent and in Polynesia, the black people in Africa, the white people in Europe, and the red race in the Americas. This is not a precise scientific description, but there was an evident segregation of the peoples of the earth. We cannot say how far this was intended to be perpetuated, since we do not know of any scripture which speaks to this subject.

Was not Israel commanded to keep segregated from other na- 292
tions, and would not this teach that national or racial segregation
is God's will for us?

Actually that is not a true parallel. In Israel the segregation was for religious rather than racial or social reasons. God called Abraham to live apart from the nations of the earth and promised that through his posterity all the nations of the earth would be blessed. This related to the Messiah, but there were other promises also which involved the entire nation and which required their segregation. The parallel today is not racial segregation but the command to Christians not to enter voluntarily into an unequal union between believers and unbelievers (2 Co 6:14-18). We may add that this command is often violated by those who strongly advocate racial segregation.

293 If intermarriage is entered into, is any particular combination more or less acceptable than another?

Human beings have intermarried in almost all possible color combinations as well as from varied national and social backgrounds. We know of no biblical instructions with regard to the matter. We should be clear that there is no biological obstacle, and it is a false assumption that the children of parents of different nationalities or social or political variances are impaired in any way other than socially. In the matter of *social* relationships sometimes differences in nationality will cause lack of cordiality in families, even where there is no other reason for objection to the marriage. Sometimes the marriage of a child of wealthy parents to a child of poor parents has caused unhappiness, though often this can be overcome with patience and considerateness. Human emotions are unpredictable and are not always the result of logic or justice. Prejudice can be a dominating factor, though other considerations sometimes overcome this.

294 Would you recommend "mixed marriages" between persons of diverse racial backgrounds?

It is always precarious to advise another whom he should marry, since in the teaching of the Bible marriage is intended to be a permanent relationship, "until death do us part." To recommend marriage to another is to help to lead him into a yoke which he will bear henceforth. We should seek the guidance of God even where there are no apparent obstacles, for in any case there will be many adjustments to be made. We should make sure, so far as possible, that the person with whom we are to share life is the one we wish to be the mother (or father) of our children and the one with whom we can effectively serve the Lord. There may be serious incompatibility even where there is neither racial, social, political nor religious diversity.

To advocate marriage where disparity exists in any one or more of these areas of life may be to invite nonacceptance by one's family or circle of friends. Children of such marriages are often faced with traumatic psychological problems. Our purpose is not to recommend a specific marriage to anyone but to consider whether the Bible forbids marriage where such disparity exists. We believe it does not, except in the matter of marriage between a believer in Christ and a nonbeliever. The unmarried "is at liberty to be married to whom she [or he] will; only in the Lord" (1 Co 7:39). This is a plain instruction; yet many persons violate it while insisting on a restriction which Scripture does not command. What we do recommend is an earnest and honest seeking of the will of God with regard to any union with another, and especially in the matter of marriage, which is a lifelong relationship.

Does the Bible Support Capital Punishment?

Does not capital punishment violate the teaching of the Bible? 295

Quite the contrary. We are told in Romans 13:1 that human government is ordained of God for the maintenance of a peaceable and ordered society, and the verses which follow show that this includes the administration of justice, with the sword where necessary. The first authorization of human government is found in Genesis 9, and verse 6 says, "Whoso sheddeth man's blood, by man shall his blood be shed." So the authorization to take the life of those committing certain crimes, such as murder, has existed from the beginning of human experience. Before the flood, when there appears to have been no organized government and justice was left to individuals, a chaotic condition developed.

All through the books of Moses we find the penalty of death attaching to various crimes against God and humanity. The Bible takes the position that human life comes from God and that the sentence of physical death (as well as spiritual death) is His penalty for sin. We read in the New Testament that by one man sin entered into the world, and death by sin, and that consequently death has passed upon all men, because all have sinned (Ro 5:12). Normally God sets the duration of each person's life, as we read in Job 14:5: "Seeing his [man's] days are determined, the number of his months are with thee." In His wisdom He varies the length of life, and none may ask Him, "What doest thou?" (Dan 4:35). Murder is viewed as an intrusion into the prerogative of God as well as being the ultimate crime against the one whose life has been taken. Anyone who commits this crime— or others which are specified in Scripture—forfeits his own right to live.

296 In opposing capital punishment some have called it legalized murder. Is this a fair statement?

It most certainly is not. Such an accusation constitutes a contradiction of terms. The dictionary defines murder as: "the offense of unlawfully killing a human being with malice aforethought, express or implied." The execution of those whose crimes fall within the categories prescribed by law is not murder, though men's ideas of which crimes are worthy of death may vary according to the circumstances of life. What is considered a capital crime in one set of circumstances may not be thought so in another. Numerous crimes which were subject to the death penalty in the Mosaic economy are not so dealt with in later times. This does not necessarily mean that the crimes are now less heinous in the sight of God, but rather the penalty prescribed shows His estimate of the extent of the guilt involved, even though He does not deal with all mankind on that basis.

297 Does not the New Testament reveal God as a God of love, and does not this alter the Old Testament teaching?

It is a fallacy to suppose that the character of God has changed and that, whereas He was a God of vengeance in the Old Testament, He is a God of love in the New. Since "God is love," as we read in 1 John 4:8, He was, and must always have been, that— whether in Old Testament or New Testament times. His character cannot change. The New Testament, equally with the Old, shows that God is a God of vengeance. We have, for example, in Romans 12:19, "Vengeance is mine; I will repay, saith the Lord"; and in Hebrews 12:29, "For our God is a consuming fire." There may have been a greater emphasis on justice in the Old Testament and on love in the New, but both characteristics are clearly portrayed in both. There is a progressive revelation in the Bible of God's will and purposes, but no later revelation was ever for the correction of something previously revealed.

What was the purpose of progressive revelation?   298

It was needful because of the dense spiritual darkness into which men fell through sin. When men forsook the living God and rebelled against Him, their feelings and desires and their mode of thinking became perverted. For God to have brought them at once into the full blaze of the light of His truth and His presence would have blasted them with judgment. It was in God's forbearance that He painstakingly revealed His truth at various times and in various measures, as we read in Hebrews 1:1. God's decrees and acts of judgment brought men to see their sinful condition and to understand His love by His provision for their redemption. These things are not meant to be matters of controversy, and if we study them in that spirit we shall fail to understand God's purposes in it all. But if we study the Scripture in a spirit of meekness, the Holy Spirit will lead us, for "the meek will he guide in judgment: and the meek will he teach his way" (Ps 25:9).

How can we reconcile the Golden Rule with capital punishment?   299

The one is personal, the other governmental. The confusion of these two aspects has resulted in our permissive society, in which often the criminal finds greater protection from penalty than the public finds from being preyed on by the criminal elements of society. Many have thought that the Bible teaches permissiveness, but the purpose of governmental decrees is to show that grace reigns through righteousness "by Jesus Christ our Lord" (Ro 5:21). When we ignore God and Christ and omit righteousness and still emphasize love, the result is the establishment of sin and violence.

The Golden Rule, "As ye would that men should do to you, do ye also to them likewise" (Lk 6:31), was given to Christ's disciples as a rule for their personal lives. It was never meant to be made the rule for dealing with criminals. Part of God's purpose in establishing human government was the suppression of crime, taking it out of the hands of individuals. When justice was administered by "the avenger of the blood," it was easy to have a miscarriage of justice. By making it a governmental function the killer was assured of a fair trial to determine whether or not he was guilty. But Scripture nowhere suggests that the penalty should not be carried out if he were found guilty of murder—unless there were special circumstances which warranted this. Thus the rights of the accused were secured, and society was protected against the depredations of wicked and violent persons. There is no need to reconcile the Golden Rule and capital punishment. The one is the rule for normal Christian living; the other is God's appointed way of dealing with capital crimes and those who commit them.

Can War Be Justified from the Bible?

300 Is war a relic of barbarism, or can it be justified from the Bible?

I would suggest an alteration of terms. Often our ideas, and consequently our ideals, are formed by the terminology we use. By the term "barbarism" we get a picture of primitive man at an early stage of evolutionary struggle upward, and we may think of war as part of his struggle toward an organized society. Such a picture is totally at variance with the teaching of the Bible, which is that violence and rapacity are the fruits of sin, resulting from man's rebellion against God.

In the Old Testament it is clear that God permitted war, and He is even said to have fought on the side of His people, by giving them providential help. In Deuteronomy 1:30 Moses promised the people of Israel that when they invaded the land of Canaan the Lord *would* fight for them; and in Joshua 10:14 we are told that He did so. Some of Israel's wars were commanded by God. On one occasion David inquired, "Shall I go and smite these Philistines?" and the Lord answered, "Go, and smite the Philistines, and save Keilah," a city of Judah (1 Sa 23:2). In 2 Samuel 5:19 is recorded a similar circumstance on a later occasion. It is apparent that we cannot say that all wars are condemned in the Bible.

How does the Bible explain the causes of war?   301

There are various causes of war, and it has been remarked that as long as nations have armaments and conflicting interests, we shall always find the strong oppressing the weak. Sometimes there are genuine differences of opinion as to the rightness or wrongness of certain claims, but when the feelings of men are aroused to a certain pitch, an action is taken which one nation considers to be the conservation of their rights but which another nation considers an encroachment on *their* rights. Such matters soon cease to be reasoned, and it becomes a contest of strength.

The epistle of James indicates that a moral condition underlies such struggles: "From whence come wars and fightings among you? come they not hence, even of your lusts that war in your members? Ye lust, and have not: ye kill, and desire to have, and cannot obtain: ye fight and war, yet ye have not, because ye ask not. Ye ask, and receive not, because ye ask amiss, that ye may consume it upon your lusts" (4:1-3). War is simply the extension of the crime and violence which occur in every nation. When men's hearts are not right with God they settle things without recourse to principles of righteousness.

What biblical basis can there be for war today?   302

There is an underlying principle of government which justifies war under certain conditions. Obviously not all wars are equally just or necessary, and some may be distinctively unjust. Romans 13 discusses the place of human government in society, and it is there stated that the government becomes God's minister or agent to regulate life in its normal aspects and to put down crime and criminals. The same principle covers international relationships.

Normal international relationships are governed by treaties and agreements, and there are even conventions of war to which many nations have subscribed, though these are often violated in actual warfare. Sometimes one nation molests the citizens of another nation or in some way invades their rights and well-being and the offended nation feels it necessary to fight to preserve its integrity and the welfare of its citizens. This is similar to when a man's house is broken into and he calls the sheriff or other law officer for protection and perhaps redress. The principle is the same but executed on a larger scale. When there has been an open attack by another nation, almost everyone recognizes the victim's right to self-defense.

303 Is killing in warfare any different from murder?

Yes, the circumstances are entirely different. The Bible records many accounts of warfare, but in no case is it ever referred to as murder. The one apparent exception was when David deliberately had Uriah put in the forefront of the battle in order that he might be killed by the Ammonites. Here it was not strictly an act of war but rather conspiracy to achieve the death of Uriah. The prophet Nathan told David, "Thou hast killed Uriah the Hittite . . . with the sword of the children of Ammon" (2 Sa 12:9). In no other case is a death in warfare called murder, and we believe it is a misconstruction of the teaching of the Bible to describe it so in our day.

This does not mean the fact of being at war justifies personal crimes or atrocities. These are always condemned, and whenever there is a personal act of violence not necessary to the proper conduct of war, it is still prosecuted as the crime it is. There are certain conventions of war which were intended to prevent unnecessary suffering on the part of civilian populations, though since World War 1, when treaties were considered by some to be "mere scraps of paper," these conventions have been largely ignored. In all-out warfare civilian populations are attacked as well as troops and military installations, though even yet it is considered an atrocity to attack a defenseless civilian population where no military objective is involved. But it is not the teaching of the Bible that warfare itself is equivalent to murder.

304 Is a Christian justified in participating in warfare?

There are widely divergent views about this. Some think a Christian should refuse any participation, though it is difficult to escape that if we have any part at all in our modern complex economy. Others believe we can accept service as a noncombatant, perhaps in the medical or signal corps, or in any activity acceptable to the draft board which does not bring us into actual combat with opposed forces. This should not be dismissed as an act of cowardice. Many who are in some form of noncombative service are exposed to more danger than others who are part of the fighting force. Many others, however, feel that since the government is charged with the defense and well-being of the country, it is improper to require them to use only the non-Christian part of the population but that all should share in this responsibility as occasion may require and where it can be done without violating one's conscience.

All of us, I am sure, regret the necessity for warfare and desire peace so far as it is possible within the framework of liberty and justice for all.

How Did the Different Races of Humanity Originate?

It is widely held that the black race came into being through 305 Noah's curse on his son Ham. Does the Bible support this?

No, it does not. The incident referred to is found in Genesis 9, where we read that Noah, possibly through ignorance of the effects of fermented wine, became drunk. Apparently his son Ham in some way dishonored his father who, in spite of his condition, knew what Ham had done. When he was recovered from his drunkenness Noah pronounced a curse, not on Ham but on Ham's son Canaan. We do not know the circumstances and believe that God has purposely left them in obscurity.

The substance of the curse was, "a servant of servants shall he be unto his brethren" (v. 25). This says nothing of any color distinction. It is true that *Ham* means "dark" or "swarthy," but not all descendants of Ham were black, although all black people are believed to have descended from Ham. The name Ham, in a slightly different form, was used for Egypt. One of Ham's sons was named *Cush*, which means "black," and his name was given to Ethiopia or Abyssinia. It is believed that the black race may have sprung from him, although not all his descendants were black.

As to Canaan, upon whom Noah's curse rested specifically, we know of no reason to think his posterity were black. Genesis 10:15-20 locates the descendants of Canaan in the land called by his name, otherwise known as Palestine from the Philistines. These nations, descended from Canaan, became so degraded and depraved that when the Israelites were later given that land, Joshua was commanded to kill all the inhabitants.

With regard to slavery, there is no indication that black people were held as slaves in ancient times. Rather, it was the custom of the strong to oppress the weak, and captives taken in wars were held as slaves. This prevailed among whites and blacks, whites making other whites their slaves and blacks making other blacks their slaves. Slavery was common among ancient peoples without regard to color. The enslavement of blacks by whites is a comparatively recent phenomenon, except in a few cases, and the trade was participated in by both blacks and whites. There is no indication that slavery was confined to the descendants of either Ham or his son Canaan.

306 Some have thought that the black race is descended from Cain. Is this biblical?

This has no foundation whatever. In the first place, the mark was put on Cain to keep men from killing him, marking him out in some way as the object of God's judgment so that men would fear to take his life. We are not told what this mark was. Had it been a black skin (for which we see no authority in the Bible), this would have been eliminated at the time of the flood, since at that time the entire human race was destroyed except the family of Noah. Since Noah came from the line of Seth, whom God raised up in place of Abel, there were no descendants of Cain on earth after the flood.

307 If the races did not originate with Cain or with the curse of Noah on his grandson Canaan, how did they originate?

The Bible does not tell us specifically how the different color races came into being, but we are told that all men came originally from Adam and later from the family of Noah. This means that all humanity is essentially, after the flesh, one family. We are told in Acts 17:26 that God "hath made of one blood all nations of men for to dwell on all the face of the earth," which confirms the fact that the human race is essentially *one*.

Does the Bible give any idea as to how the races came into being? 308

While the Bible does not tell us how the color races came into being, it does give an account of the origin of the different languages of humanity, and the two may be related. We are told in Genesis 11 that up to the time of the building of the tower of Babel humanity lived as one great community, all speaking the same language. Since the time was not long after the flood, the population would have been comparatively small. The building of this tower seems to have been an act of rebellion against God, and God dealt with this action and attitude by dividing humanity into different groups. In the Bible, this is related to the inauguration of language differences, but it could very well be that other distinctions were introduced at the same time, for shortly after that we have men of different races, distinguished not only by language but by certain physical characteristics also, including differing color.

Some have thought that these physical changes were the result of differing climatic conditions throughout the world, but there are serious difficulties with regard to this. Comparable climatic conditions have not resulted in the same physical changes, nor in the same colors. There seems to have been a physical change in the genes of men, comparable to the change in their language, which was by an act of God and not a gradual development, according to the biblical record. Further, there came into being not only the white and black races but also the brown, yellow, and red. Nor is there any way of knowing the original color of man. Some think the name Adam is a variant of Edom, which means "red." It could be that man's original color was red, or ruddy, and not "paleface," as the American Indian called the European intruders into his domain.

What is clear in the Bible is that all humanity had a common ancestor, and the New Testament makes this fact part of its doc-

trine. All men are said to be "in Adam" by natural birth, and so
we are "by nature the children of wrath" (Eph 2:3) because
Adam had transgressed God's commandment before any children
were born to him. The sinfulness of human nature is seen in
Adam's first son, who became a murderer and a liar, while his
second son, Abel, became a spiritual child of God through faith,
as we read in Hebrews 11:4. Further we are told that Christ
died for all (1 Ti 2:5-6), which means that God's salvation is
open to all men, of whatever language or color. Also every believer in Christ is united to Him and to every other believer in
one spiritual body, according to Ephesians 4:4, so that we are
"all one in Christ Jesus" (Gal 3:28). And this is by grace, through
faith in Christ, without other distinction.

What Is the Biblical Attitude Toward Space Exploration?

**309 Does the Bible condemn space exploration and interplanetary
travel?**

There is a verse in the Bible which some have thought condemns space exploration. This is Psalm 115:16: "The heaven,
even the heavens, are the LORD's: but the earth hath he given to
the children of men." However, we do not believe this is intended to limit the extent of man's research. The context suggests a
sequence of thought—that the heavens are the sphere particularly
of the Lord's activities, i.e., of angel hosts, and the earth is the
sphere of man's activities. The passage goes on to speak of the
dead as those removed from the sphere of human experience; and
then it apparently looks beyond the grave to the fact that death
does not end the conscious joy of believers, but rather ushers them
into a state where they can praise God without restraint. I doubt
that the passage is intended to inhibit space exploration.

But apart from any biblical injunction, man has a built-in
inhibitory system which, while it may not prevent his arriving at
a distant planet, could possibly keep him from being established

on it. Human life is geared to the environment in which we live, and while man has been able to spend some days in a space ship and also to live for a considerable time under water, this requires the establishment of certain environmental conditions without which human life would cease. Human life is geared to certain conditions of gravity, air mixture and pressure, temperature and other tolerances which, if they are varied in any appreciable degree, could produce not only discomfort but even death. Consequently, to become established on some heavenly body would require environmental conditions which presumably would have to be constructed, unless there is another planet which has conditions similar to those of earth.

If men do reach any other planet, does the Bible indicate whether 310
they will find life-forms, especially any type of being similar to
man?

This question is often raised. In my thinking the answer lies not so much in speculation about what may exist "out there" as it does in what the Bible says about man. We are told that man is made in the image of God, and there are some theological implications in this which seem to me to preclude the existence of other beings comparable to man. And this applies even more to redemption. It would have been an easy matter for God to have created beings on other planets comparable to man in intelligence, suited to whatever environment may exist on such a planet. And there would be no problem with regard to such beings having endless existence as man has.

The problem lies in the matter of redemption. The Bible tells us that the wages of sin is death, and redemption can only be provided by the payment of that penalty. Scripture teaches also that even those who die in their sins have endless existence and therefore any atonement must be infinite in nature. But an infinite atonement can be accomplished only by an infinite person, giving infinite value to any act performed. Only God is infinite. This is why our redemption required the incarnation of Christ; not that incarnation achieved redemption, but the fact of the infinite God becoming man made possible a death which had infinite value; and it was this which purchased our redemption.

If other beings comparable to man exist on other planets, then if they have sinned, would God desire their redemption? But this would require an incarnation of Christ in their nature, whereas the Bible teaches that when Christ died and rose again for our salvation, He did not cease to be man but retains His human as well as His divine life. The apostle Paul wrote: "For there is one God, and one mediator between God and men, the man Christ Jesus; who gave himself a ransom for all, to be testified in due time" (1 Ti 2:5-6). This makes it unlikely if not impossible for Christ to have assumed the nature of any other kind of being, since He is called "the *man* Christ Jesus."

It may be argued that there could be such a race of beings who have not sinned and who do not need redemption, but if that were true, why did God create *two* races of beings in His image, knowing that one would sin and require the incarnation and subsequent death of His Son? It seems to me that to argue for the existence of beings similar to man on other planets overlooks God's purposes in creation and the fact that God has identified Himself with man, not only in creation but far more in redemption. In other words, as a matter of scientific speculation we might assume the possibility of the existence of creatures similar to man in the universe, but theological considerations would rule this out.

311 Could there be other forms of life in which creatures would have intelligence comparable to man without man's peculiar relationship to God?

There could, of course, be such forms of life, although if God is satisfied that such a condition should prevail elsewhere, it might be asked why such a condition should not be acceptable on earth? The entire speculation, it seems to me, arises from leaving out of the picture God and His divine purposes both in creation and redemption.

312 If the other planets are not inhabited, what purpose could be served by the creation of so many of them?

The Bible has a great deal to say about creation as a witness to God's existence and also to His wisdom and power. One classic passage is Psalm 19:1-6:

The heavens declare the glory of God; and the firmament showeth his handywork. Day unto day uttereth speech, and night unto night sheweth knowledge. There is no speech nor language, where their voice is not heard. Their line is gone out through all the earth, and their words to the end of the world. In them hath he set a tabernacle for the sun, which is as a bridegroom coming out of his chamber, and rejoiceth as a strong man to run a race. His going forth is from the end of the heaven, and his circuit unto the ends of it: and there is nothing hid from the heat thereof.

God is glorified in His works, and the extent of creation bespeaks the infinity of its Creator.

Is a Classless Society Biblical?

Communism often identifies capitalism with Christianity and condemns both. What does the Bible say on this subject? 313

In the Bible God deals chiefly with men's relationship with Himself, though He has much to say about interpersonal relationships also. When God ordained that men should live by the sweat of their face (Gen 3:19), there were few people on earth. Life was simple and chiefly agrarian. Life was a struggle for existence, and men required the help of others for special tasks, especially when harvesting grain. Some gave themselves to the raising of cattle, and there was some trade and barter. Later some became artisans, and their services were secured by value payments. Perhaps originally payment was made in goods, but a monetary system was devised to facilitate trade. One might furnish goods or services for money to be used at a later time in an entirely different exchange.

Some persons worked hard and lived frugally, and these built up a monetary reserve. Others lived more lavishly, or perhaps did not work as hard. They enjoyed pleasure, perhaps even luxury, but did not have a monetary reserve. Commercial transactions led to economic distinctions. These were not essentially wrong.

314 What does the Bible say about economic relationships?

The Bible deals with the moral and spiritual aspects of these things. The problems of social relationships do not arise from the system of granting to each the fruit of his toil, with the concurrent right to live frugally and lay up a store against a time of sickness or other adversity. So long as men deal honestly this system enables large numbers of persons to deal and share with one another equitably. But sin leads some to neglect duty, and leads others to make exorbitant charges for goods or services. An artificial system is built up, widening the gap between those who have and those who have not. This has led to social classes wherever men are found.

The Word of God condemns sinful indulgences and the equally sinful injustices which many practice. It condemns exploitation, but not the right to hold property earned by diligence and skill. Through various circumstances some countries are rich, though containing many poor. Other countries are characteristically poor, though containing many who are rich, some fabulously so. This is partly due to natural circumstances, but the condition indicates the need for corrective measures.

315 Does not the Bible condemn the rich?

Not per se. The Bible condemns avarice, covetousness, and miserliness. First Timothy 6 speaks of the evil of setting one's heart on the acquisition of riches. Such an attitude can "drown men in . . . perdition," and leads to temptations and snares. A literal rendering of verse 10 is: "The love of money is a root of all kinds of evil." It should be noted that it does not say this of money, but of the love of it.

The Bible discusses interpersonal relationships. Servants are exhorted to serve their employers faithfully, with good will, honoring Christ (Eph 6:5-8; Col 3:22-25). God promises to recompense their services. Employers are reminded that they have a Master in heaven to whom they must give account. They should therefore be just and considerate in their treatment of employees. And beyond all this is the golden rule: "Therefore all things whatsoever ye would that men should do to you, do ye even so to them" (Mt 7:12). We have an illustration of a good relationship between employer and employees in the book of Ruth, where Boaz, a wealthy man, said to those who reaped his field, "The LORD be with you." The men replied, "The LORD bless thee" (Ru 2:4).

Relating to commerce, much is said in the Bible about honest weight and true measures. There must be honesty in business dealings. "A false balance is abomination to the LORD: but a just weight is his delight" (Pr 11:1). Where prices are hiked not because of greater value, but merely to make added profit, God is highly displeased.

What about the verse in James: "Go to now, ye rich men, weep 316 and howl for your miseries that shall come upon you" (Ja 5:1)?

Since the rich have often oppressed the poor throughout human history, this is a prophecy that the time would come when God, by His providential overruling of human affairs, would reverse the situation. It is not essentially a condemnation of the monetary system, but of the abuse of it. Nor does it suggest that all rich persons are cruel and oppressive. Many are genuinely philanthropic, and consider their possessions a trust from God. This Scripture may be finding some measure of fulfillment today.

In the Old Testament the Hebrew word for *rich* signifies "heavy," implying that riches are a burden. There may be the implication also that riches hinder spiritual exercise. Matthew Henry makes this comment on riches: "There is a burden of care in getting them, fear in keeping them, temptation in using them, guilt in abusing them, sorrow in losing them, and a burden of account, at last, to be given up concerning them." In God's sight riches are a stewardship to be administered under His direction.

What does the Bible teach about property rights?   317

The Bible discusses both the acquisition of property and the disposition of it in 1 Timothy 6. There is spiritual danger in an inordinate desire to increase one's possessions. In Luke 12 the Lord Jesus warns against allowing our possessions to possess us. The Bible recognizes property rights, but condemns covetousness, hoarding, and miserliness. Covetousness is declared to be idolatry (Col 3:5; Eph 5:5). Hoarding implies lack of faith in God to provide for one's future. We believe it is right for us to provide for expected needs, and it is right for parents to help their children (2 Co 12:14). But the Lord Jesus makes it clear that laying up treasure in heaven involves corresponding sacrifice of earthly values (Mt 6:19-24).

We ought to be seeking ways in which we can serve God by ministering to the welfare of others. "Whoso hath this world's good, and seeth his brother have need, and shutteth up his bowels of compassion from him, how dwelleth the love of God in him?" (1 Jn 3:17). To love our neighbor as ourself requires that we have concern about his needs. This by no means teaches the equalization of wealth. Too many factors are involved to make this feasible. Yet the Lord called that man a fool who lived unto himself (Lk 12:16-22). He said, "So is he that layeth up treasure for himself, and is not rich toward God," putting the matter on a moral and spiritual level, rather than thinking of it merely as a social obligation.

TOPICAL INDEX

(See also the Table of Contents)

SCRIPTURE INDEX

220